You Just Have To Laugh
Publishing

You Just Have to Laugh Publishing
Lenexa, Kansas U.S.A.
youjusthavetolaugh.com or naster.com
Printed by Wasworth Printing

2 4 6 8 10 9 7 5 3 1

First Printing: 2016 March
Library of Congress Catalog Number: 2008930379
ISBN: 096631459X

The purpose of this book is to educate and entertain. The author and You Just Have to Laugh Publishing shall have neither liability nor responsibility to any person or entity with respect to any loss or damage caused, or alleged to be caused, directly or indirectly by the information contained in this guidebook.

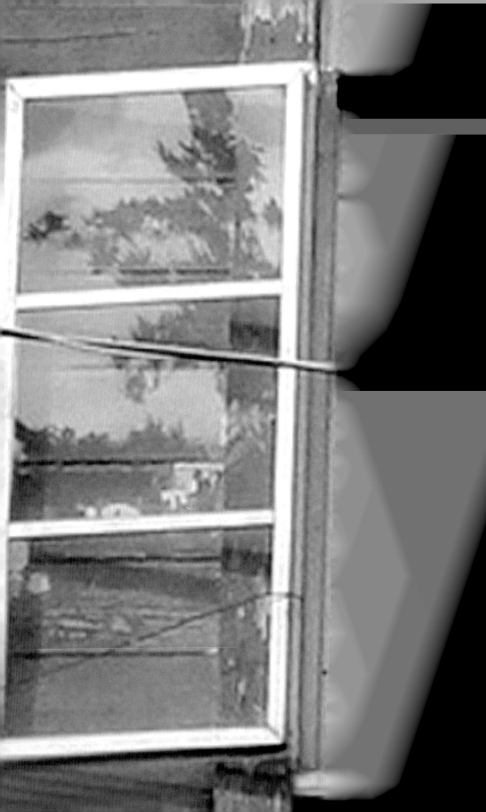

CHAPTERS

You Just Have to Laugh

... is simply how humor makes tough times better. It's intentions are:

To Offer joy

To Create laughter

To Serve humanity

To Live the example

To Help those in need

It is my sincere wish this manual will guide and help you through your tough times bringing joy and happiness.

David Naster

You Just Have To Laugh

YJHTL's MISSION

To illustrate the monumental value humor & laughter brings in life's TOUGHEST TIMES

We all go through tough times. Some are rougher than others. And such moments cloud our ability to live a joyful life.

When we experience the darkness of fear, sadness or anger, the thought of, "I may never be happy again" haunts our hearts and souls.

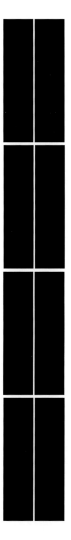
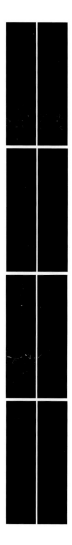

During such moments we need to remove the darkness. Humor and laughter are the windows we open to let the light in. It shines brighteness through any dark cloud. And that divine light brings us to a joyful and happy life - through any tough time.

Chapter 1

HUMOR
&
LAUGHTER

Humor

... is the quality of something being amusing. Humor is also thinking funny, which causes amusement. This joyous cycle leads to

LAUGHTER

... the effect of humor.

Only **U**
can connect them.

The TRUTH
is best understood
in a STORY

YJHTL

is
Real Stories
from
Real People
with
Real Problems
that are
Real Funny

HUMOR
is created by:

WORD PLAY >
multiple meaning of words

ABSURDITY >
ridiculous & laughable

DISTORTION >
to twist, stretch, exaggerate

Legendary comedian Bob Hope proved to be funny right up to the end. With not long to live, his wife, Dolores, asked him where he would like to be buried.

Bob said, "Surprise me."

Julie, "Mom was in hospice and was becoming delirious. She constantly complained about hysterectomy pain. I finally told her she never had one.

"'I did, too,' mom said. 'You wouldn't remember. It happened before you were born.'"

Doug had his legs and all but two fingers amputated because of diabetes. The disability company sent Doug a letter asking if he was really disabled. Doug had a friend take a picture of him with shorts on. He sent the picture to the insurance company with the caption: "What do YOU think?"

Humor

helps

manage

EMOTIONS

FEAR

Scott Burton: "Part of surviving cancer comes down to fear and learning how to handle it. Fear is what sets us off in search of humor. Once you see the profound seriousness in life, you can truly recognize the beauty of humor.

"After my fourth surgery, the simplest touch would send my foot twitching out of control. For fun, I'd show people. Watch this! (Letting my foot go crazy.) I was like a kid with a new toy.

"The first time my brother visited me in the hospital, I was explaining my prostate exam. He was uncomfortable I said, 'Wow, my first prostate exam. Are they supposed to use a puppet?'"

"Cancer didn't stop me from being funny."

SADNESS

Audrey, "I loved my dad and miss him. But I have the most amazing memories and funny stories to remember him by.

"My mom would always blame daddy if anything went wrong or got messed up. She did this their entire marriage. It got to be a joke when something went wrong, 'daddy must have done it.'

"It was no surprise that it continued even when daddy got sick. One night we had a storm blow through and the power shut off. After a few seconds the power came back on. Daddy yelled from his hospital bed, 'I didn't touch anything.'

"Later that night, I tucked him in and he turned his Batman flashlight on and was humming and doing circles on the ceiling, giggling and whispering, 'Ha Ha, it wasn't my fault.'"

ANGER

Lloyd, "I was in the hospital with an abscessed pancreas and a temperature of 104. The doctor said I was going to be fine. Later, I overheard him telling my family I might not make it. I was furious.

"The next time I heard the doctor coming down the hall, I pulled the sheet over my head. The doc walked in. I heard him gasp. My plan worked. He thought I was dead. As he pulled the sheet back, I yelled, 'BOO!'

"I got him.

"After we laughed, I insisted the doctor be honest with me and get down to the business of making me feel better."

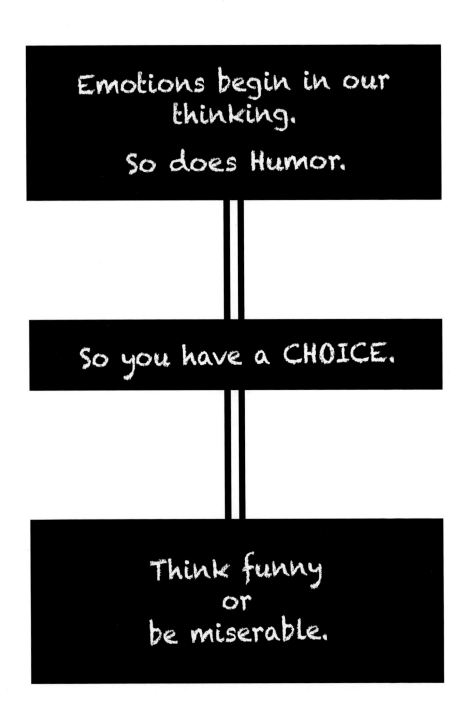

Julia,
"Katie, my beloved cocker spaniel, died after 15 years. I had her cremated and kept the ashes in my living room.

"When mom died, we had her cremated as well. After the service, my best friend Tonya asked, 'Where are you going to put your mom?'

"'In the living room,' I said, 'next to Katie. That way, I can have both my bitches right next to one another.'"

Chapter 2

Laughing
at
YOURSELF

The ability to laugh at yourself is one of the greatest gifts you can give yourself. As a parent, it is one of the most important survival skills we can teach our kids.

When you laugh at what you think is wrong with you, you become superior to it. Any feelings of hurt, anger or even sadness do not own you anymore.

When you laugh at yourself, you recognize your humanity. You are not perfect. You make mistakes. And you're like everybody else.

That simple understanding makes you compassionate to others. Recognizing we are alike and laughing together connects us at the deepest level.

David

Removing Shame

Accepting who you are, loving who you are, finding joy in who you are removes any painful feelings of humiliation, distress or that something is wrong with you.

Self-Esteem

Another great by-product of laughing at yourself is self-esteem. When you respect yourself for who you truly are - including all of your flaws, shortcomings and mistakes -

YOU FEEL GREAT ABOUT YOURSELF

and

No One Can Take That Away from You!

Paul Hill was a highway patrolman for the State of Colorado. Shooting radar one day, Paul clocked a Jaguar doing 80 miles an hour. The posted speed limit was 55.

Paul, "I approached the left side of the car and asked to see a license and registration. I told the man he was speeding. He insisted he was not. I explained the radar gun showed 80 miles per hour. The man was adamant, saying, 'Officer, I was not driving 80 miles per hour.'

"As I leaned in the window to confront him, I realized the Jaguar was an English model. The steering wheel was on the right side. I was talking to the passenger, who indeed was not driving 80 mph. In fact, he wasn't driving at all.

"Laughing, I said, 'Sir, you are correct. You were not driving 80. Sorry for the inconvenience and have a nice day.'

"I got in my car and drove off."

RAGS SMITH

" I always incorporated my real life experiences to teach my students. One summer, I was shopping for a pick-up truck. While looking around the lot, a salesman approached. He began talking. He stuttered.

"While I admired his courage, I wondered why a stutterer would choose a profession where he talks for a living.

"The salesman handed me his business card. Printed prominently under the name of the dealership was his name. The card read:

B-B-B-Bill W-W-W-Whiteside

"I looked up. He was smiling. We laughed. I bought my truck from Bill. The following Christmas, my family received a card from him. The greeting read:

M-M-M-MERRY C-C-C-HRISTMAS
B-B-B-BILL"

Mrs. Clifton

"**I**n my first year of teaching, the most challenging class came in the last hour of the school day. Teaching high school psychology is hard enough, but when the room is filled with members of the varsity football team, your work is cut out for you.

"The first week of school the team was going through twice-a-day workouts. By the time they got to my last-hour class, these guys would fall asleep.

"Finally, I ran out of patience and lost it. I started yelling, ending my short tirade with, 'Since all of you like sleeping so much, you can all just sleep with me after school!'

"I was so mad, I didn't realized my gaffe. The students did. And they were howling.

"No one ever slept in my class again. They wanted to hear what I might say next."

72-Year-Old Emma

"**O**ne day a policeman pulled me over for speeding. I was guilty, but didn't want a ticket. Who would? As the officer approached, I started moving rapidly from side to side. He noticed and asked if I was all right. I said I had to use the toilet, and a woman my age can't hold it very easily.

"I didn't have to use the toilet, but I needed an excuse to get out of that speeding ticket. The officer believed me and said to drive the speed limit to the nearest bathroom.

"As I drove off, I laughed at my prank. The more I thought about it, the harder I laughed. Soon I was laughing so hard, I really did have to pee. That made me laugh even more. Finally, I was laughing so hard, I went. I pulled over. Not because I wet myself.

"My teeth had fallen onto my lap."

Another story from Doug

My dear friend, Dave, is short. I always teased him about his height. After I got my legs amputated because of diabetes.. I called Dave and said,

"Hey, I just had my legs cut off but I'm still taller than you."

Sarah

"I don't make 'mistakes.' When I goof up, it's called a 'scientific experiment.' Once, I left my husband's sunroof open during a thunderstorm. I told him it was an experiment. My conclusion: The driver's seat of a Honda Accord will hold 20 gallons of water.

"Another time, I left my car door open while backing out of the garage. My conclusion: That a car door going 5 mph will push a file cabinet through a garage wall, leaving a three-foot hole."

LAUGHING at MYSELF

... frees me of any shame, worthlessness or thinking something is wrong with me. None of that is true.

I am simply ME.

David

Chapter 3

Illness
&
Injury

I cannot make any sense of why children get abused, people endure horrible illnesses, and innocent folks suffer unnecessarily.

Life can be far from just, equal, kind, reasonable and easy. But those are all a part of life. Just as joy, happiness and fun can be.

We all must be able to find that passageway from bad time to a good time. Humor and laughter can be that road.

They may not fix the problem, but they can make a bad time not as bad. When we can find some humor in a tough time, it loosens the noose of paralyzing emotions that will suffocate our life.

David

Think funny

Be miserable

Permission to LAUGH

Living in FEAR

The CHOICE is Yours

"I was asked to perform at a back clinic with patients dealing with Level 10 back pain. I started off with, 'Hi, I'm David and I'm an alcoholic. Oops, wrong meeting.' And I ran out.

"This brought surprisingly loud laughter. For the next 10 minutes, I hit them with my sure-fire funny stuff. Once I had them laughing, I asked the group to call out reasons why Level 10 pain is good.

"The room fell silent. Everyone stared at me. After an a long, awkward pause, a man yelled, 'No responsibility!'

People laughed.

"A woman said, 'You get to sleep all day.'

'24-hour room service!' another added.

"More laughter!

"Somebody called, 'More drugs!'

"The room erupted with laughter."

"Voices grew louder as they got more involved. People, who were once frowning, were laughing out loud. A woman in too much pain to sit up when the meeting started, was now perched on the edge of her chair. The biggest laugh of the day was when the oldest woman in the room said, 'The best thing about being at level 10 is that it is a better excuse than telling my husband I have a headache!'

"The LAUGHTER was tremendous.

"We did a quick check. Every person in that room had a lower pain level."

David

Alzheimers

Sally Balot was worried she had Alzheimer's disease. She asked her grandson, Rich, to take her to the family doctor.

Rich, "At the doctor's office, grandma explained why she was afraid she was losing her memory – describing her symptoms.

"The doctor patiently sat and listened to grandma. After she finished talking, the doctor folded his hands, leaned across the table and said, 'You know what, Sally, I'd just forget about it.'

"Grandma and I were speechless. The doctor broke out into a huge smile. He assured us there was nothing to worry about.

"'Just forget about it' became grandma's ongoing joke."

Dementia

Jerry, "My Uncle Lou has Dementia. Father's Day, the family gathered in the kitchen. One of the grandkids started singing 'Old McDonald Had a Farm.'

"With every animal sang, Uncle Lou made the sound of that animal, repeating the name. So, when the kid sang, 'on that farm he had some cows,' Uncle Lou would say 'cows,' and then make a long, drawn-out mooing sound.

"I think every animal on Noah's Ark was mentioned. But Uncle Lou was enjoying himself, not doing any harm, so nothing was said.

"When the song finally ended, everyone applauded. The boy's aunt said, 'There sure were a lot of animals on Old McDonald's farm.'

"Uncle Lou slapped the table, stood up and hollered, 'It's his damn farm. He can have as many animals as he damn well pleases!'

"We laughed so hard, we had to pick our selves up off the floor."

■ ■ ■ ■ ■ ■ ■ ■ ■ ■ ■ ■ ■

Holly Dodd, "Sarcoidosis produces nodules of lumps beneath the skin. I have extremely painful nodes on my lungs, eyes and skin.

"I never whine. I've learned that complaining makes people disappear. Since I have no intention of being alone, I decided to have fun. When people ask me how I feel, I say:

"'How am I? How do you think I am? I'm in pain, you moron.'

"'And, by the way, I am not sick, I am health challenged.

"Then I went out and bought some fake 'Billy-Bob' teeth. They looked disgustingly real. I had fun with them. Before and after each of my chemo treatments, I told the nurse:

"'My mouth feels funny. My gums seem swollen and my teeth seem to be growing.' The nurse documented each complaint. After the seventh visit, she called me in her office. While her eyes were on the chart, I put in the 'Billy-Bob' teeth.

"The nurse looked up, saw my mouth and screamed. Then laughing, she had me trick three more nurses.

"We decided to fool the doctor.

"The next week I was sitting in the examining room – 'Billy-Bob' teeth in place. In walks the doctor. He sat. As he read my chart, he never looked up at me. He sounded puzzled as he mumbled, 'Teeth seem to be growing. Tingling sensation. Gums swollen?'
"When he finally looked up and saw my fake teeth, he jumped three feet, stumbling into a cabinet. Once he recovered, he said:
"'We need to radiate those teeth and stick them in your armpit. That should take care of any lymph node problems. I would also suggest flossing more often.'"

N an, "When the doctor said I would never walk again, I laughed at him. I refused to accept his diagnosis. I stayed in physical therapy for hours and hours. Even when I would fall down or didn't think I could go on, I made myself have fun.

"One time, the patients on my floor decided to get pizza. The hospital had us on strict diets. We didn't care. First, we needed to distract the nurses and all other hospital staff.

The Great Pizza Caper Team

"A paralyzed guy dialed the pizza shop using a pencil in his mouth. Next, we assembled a team to meet the delivery man downstairs. The team included me, in a wheelchair; Bob, also in a wheelchair; Mary Ann, a dwarf with stubs for legs; and Jeff, paralyzed from the waist down.

"It was a 30-minute delivery and it took us that long to sneak downstairs.

"When the pizza delivery man arrived, I told him to put all six pizzas on my lap. He said they would burn me. I laughed, explaining I was paralyzed from the waist down.

"Getting back upstairs was more difficult than getting down, since we now had pizza and sodas to contend with. As the elevator climbed, we got excited. Our plan was working. We were home free. Then, the elevator doors opened to a bunch of scowling nurses.

"They took our pizza and sodas then scolded us like children. One yelled, 'You are all grounded!'

"'Grounded?' I laughed. 'We're paralyzed!'

"If I hadn't kept finding humor and laughter, I'd still be in a wheelchair."

Pam, "My husband Tab, or 'heart-less bastard' as I affectionately call him, was complaining about vertigo. He was also throwing up a lot. The doctor prescribed a suppository.

"'Suppository?' Tab said. 'I'm not having trouble at that end.'

"It turns out Tab had a stroke. The doctor said that a hole in Tab's heart allowed a blood clot to reach his brain. My husband has a heart after all. I guess I have to change his nickname now to 'heart-ful bastard.'"

Jane,

"Dad had emergency by-pass surgery. Our family was on pins and needles. My 38-year-old sister died of colon cancer a year before. The thought of losing dad, too, was unbearable.

"The nurse told us dad made it through the operation just fine. She took us to intensive care and pointed to dad's bed. He was unrecognizable. His teeth were out; he was smothered in medical equipment. Now, add to that, bypass patients are usually swollen after surgery. It was hard to believe I was comforting my own father.

"More family members arrived. We bowed our heads, praying for dad's recovery. At that sacred moment, an ICU nurse quietly told us that the person we were praying for was not our father. Our father was on the other side of the room.

"The person we were calling 'daddy' was an 85-year-old woman."

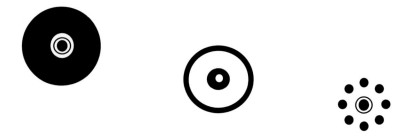

Ralph Koffman, "When my son TR, was two years old, he was diagnosed with cancer of the retina. By the time TR was eight years old, the doctor told us if they didn't remove the cancerous eye, TR would be dead within two years.

"The morning of surgery our pastor came to the hospital to lead us in prayer. Just as the pastor began, TR interrupted and said,

"'Instead of me praying to God, can we get my Sunday school teacher here, Mrs. Francis? She knows God better than I do.'

"After the successful operation, TR returned to school. His teacher did a wonderful thing. She had his entire classroom of 3rd graders all wearing an eye-patch over their right eye – the same side TR's big bandage was over.

"A month later, after TR's bandages were removed the principal called me. Apparently, TR was stealing other 3rd grader's lunch money and these kids were not eating lunch.

"When I asked TR, he insisted he wasn't stealing their money. He was simply betting the kids he could touch his tongue to his eye. When they took the bet – TR took out his fake eye and put it on his tongue.

"One time, I was taking a nap on the couch. When I awoke, TR's fake eye was stuck to my left shoulder.

"TR said, 'Watch it dad, I have my eye on you.'

"Today TR is a happy, well-adjusted 32 year-old man."

Barbara, "My support group howled when I explained how I avoid long boarding lines at airports. As soon as the first-class passengers are called, I walk to the ticket agent, pull my wig off and say 'Chemo. Bad day.'

"They have never stopped me."

Pam, "Laughing at being sick is something my grandma taught me. She had a double mastectomy. The hospital gave her a special bra. She called the bra, 'my boobs.' I will never forget the first time grandma yelled, 'Pam, I'm going to the store. Get me my boobs.'

"She wouldn't go anywhere without them, no matter what. Even when my grandpa, her husband, was rushed to the emergency room, grandma insisted we stop by the house first to:

'Pick up her boobs.'"

Julia, "My 52-year-old husband was diagnosed with prostate cancer. After surgery, his treatments consisted of large doses of female hormones. These are the same body chemicals that give women hot flashes and mood swings.

"Since my husband's body is flooded with feminine hormones, he understands me much better. He has stopped complaining about my erratic moods and hot flashes. He has them too.

"Sometimes, we have them in tandem."

Gordon, "Because of testicular cancer, I had a testicle removed. When I went back to work, the lads had a baseball and a BB sitting on my desk. One said, 'Gordon, we've organized an implant.

"'You choose the size.'"

Lorraine Beltrami

"When I was diagnosed with breast cancer, I sent an email to all my family and friends and told them of my diagnosis. I let them know I wanted no pity parties. I would only deal with cancer with humor. If they couldn't embrace that theory, I understood, but they needed to stay away. I could only deal with my emotions, not theirs.

"My cancer journey began with the making of a video using the 'Mission Impossible' theme. I also asked for people to post 'Booby' jokes and funny stuff on my blog. My theme song was 'Beat It' by Michael Jackson.

"My daughter gave me a bald party. She had all my friends cut off some of my hair before we shaved it all off. They all wore funny pink hats.

"I was lucky to have a super supportive husband and daughter. We laughed our way through two lumpectomies, chemotherapy and radiation. Today I am cancer-free. I'm thankful for the wake-up call to enjoy every minute. Not often you get a second chance in life to grab the brass ring.

Dick on surviving breast cancer: "My divorce was finalized on January 3rd. My mastectomy was on January 9th. I told people I lost three boobs in one week."

Frank, "I was 61, my wife 58, when we got married. After our honeymoon, my new bride was diagnosed with bone cancer. Her doctor said she should not expect to outlive her friends.

"We immediately went out to find her new, older friends."

Keeping it playful keeps away FEAR.

Pat Moore, "As a breast cancer patient, I not only know the value of laughing – keeping a playful attitude is just as important. I am presently going through radiation. On the opposite side of where it's given, I make tally marks as I complete each treatment. Every five marks, I make a drawing around it in wild colors. I do have an art education background.

"My intention is that my chest will become a working piece of abstract art – evolving after each treatment. My radiation doc loves it and wishes all of her patients would do this."

Carol, "My husband Bob, was 55 years old when he was diagnosed with non-Hodgkin's lymphoma. He lost his sight, ability to speak and body movement.

"Two-months into recovery I was wheeling him through the house in a wheelchair. I stopped in front of a mirror and he spoke for the first time. He looked in the mirror and said, 'Oh, so old.'

"I said, 'Honey, go easy on yourself. It's going to take a lot more time to recover. You're doing great.'

"Bob said, 'I was referring to you, not me.'"

Larry Notto, "When my mom was 68, she discovered a lump in her left breast. My sister Vicki, my brother Frank, and I were in the room with her when the oncologist came in to share the news, 'Malignant!'

"My brother, sister, and I reacted with tears. Mom told us to save them for her funeral – and that wouldn't be for a while. She then told us to be quiet and let the doctor tell her the options.

"Upon telling her of a lumpectomy, full mastectomy and the protocol that followed, mom said, 'So, if I go for the full mastectomy, the cancer will be gone? I won't have to do radiation or chemo? And I won't have to lose my hair?'

"The doctor said yes."

"Mom looked at the three of us with a gleam in her eyes and said, 'Your father has been dead since 1982. I've never dated another man since he died and don't see myself starting now. I haven't gotten any calls from Hugh Hefner or Sports Illustrated asking me to be in their magazines. I've done all the nursing I'm going to do. And I don't want to miss my hair appointments on Fridays!'

"'Doc, take it off.

"She looked back at us, laughed and said, 'Why are you all crying? I'm the one that's going to be lopsided.'"

Susie, "While I was home recovering from my mastectomy, my cousin Sharon came to visit with her mother. I love my aunt, but she is notoriously dour and humorless.

"My aunt placed her hand on my cheek and, with tears in her eyes, said sadly (as if I were notin the room),

"'Oh, and she has her Mother's eyes.'

"Sharon cracked, 'Yes she does. And now she's got her daddy's chest!'

"My aunt looked horrified. That made Sharon and I laugh even harder."

Roberta Long, "When I found out my dear friend Esther had terminal cancer, I immediately went to see her. When I asked Esther what she wanted to do with the time she had left, she said, 'travel.'

"I suggested Esther plan a trip. If she couldn't get a family member to go with her, I said I'd love to.

"Esther started to worry. She asked a bunch of 'what ifs.' 'What if I get sick?' 'What if I lose my medications?' 'What if I get lost?'

"I tried to reassure her. It didn't help. Finally, I interrupted, 'What's the worst that can happen?'

"'I could die,' Esther said,

"I smiled and said, 'Then pack your casket.'

"Esther was stunned. Finally, she smiled. Then Esther burst out laughing and didn't stop for what seemed like an hour."

Chris

"I picked up three hitchhikers outside a water park in Orlando, Florida. We were laughing and having a good time, so I offered to take them all the way to Daytona.

"A loud bang went off. Immediately, one of them wrapped something around my neck, cutting off my air supply. The guy in the front seat started steering toward the side of the road. We rolled to a stop.

"One of the guys in the back got in the driver's side, pushing me to the center of the front seat. Another slapped handcuffs on me. They drove into a marshy, wooded area. The car stopped.

"I remembered I had a knife under the seat. I grabbed it before they got me out of the car. One of them started pulling me into the woods and I stabbed his butt. With my adrenaline raging, I broke the handcuffs and pounced on him.

"Somebody jumped on my back. It felt like I was being punched. Actually, I was stabbed 16 times. I could struggle no more. They covered me with brush and tree branches, leaving me to die.

"Losing so much blood, I was barely conscious. I could hear the car start. I thought my life was over.

"Then I heard it. The car was stuck in the mud. That made me laugh. The thought of those three jerks panicking because they were stuck in a mud-hole made me laugh even harder. My laughter was distracting me from the pain. They finally drove away.

"I freed myself from the pile of brush and tree branches. Walking to the road, I kept telling myself to 'keep moving' and 'keep laughing.'

Hours Later

"I was found unconscious and taken to a hospital. The three criminals were caught and surprised to find out I was alive to identify them. After months of recovery, I went back to work.

"At first, people didn't know how to act around me. I told them that since being stabbed 16 times, I went from;

"'Chris to Swiss.'"

Injury

Sheila's leg was severed when a drunk driver hit her car. Despite wearing a prosthesis, she still plays softball and goes dancing.

Sheila has fun with her fake limb. Every Halloween, she turns it backwards and dresses it up with different shoes.

One time, Sheila and her girlfriend, Gerry, were at a nightclub. They noticed a guy strutting like God's gift to women. This guy was obnoxiously drunk – asking every woman in the bar to dance.

They all turned him down, but Mr. Wonderful wouldn't take no for an answer. He made a second round, hitting on women who had already rejected him.

The second time he came on to Sheila, she took off her leg and waved it in his face,

"Does it look like I want to dance?"

He left the club mumbling to himself.

Jack Newton was a professional golfer before he was hit by the whirling propeller of a Cessna 210. He lost his right arm, right eye and half his stomach. Jack is now a writer for Australian Golf Digest magazine.

Jack, "Writing is a time-consuming tough craft, especially when you have a glass and cigarette in your only hand."

Injury

Bobby Russo, "I was 19 years old with no worries in life. One morning, driving to work, I hit a pot-hole. My truck flipped a few times. I was thrown through the passenger side window.

"I was on the side of the interstate with a broken back. I had no lower body movement. At the hospital they discovered I had 3 broken vertebrae. After 18 hours of surgery they rebuilt me into the person (man) I am today.

"When family would come and visit in the hospital, I would put on a happy face. As soon as they left, it went away. One night after the lights were off, I looked up and asked, 'Why me?'

"I waited. Then, I laughed out loud and said, 'You idiot. No one is going to answer you!'

"From that moment on I knew my life was going to be okay. The feeling of being able to laugh is what got me out of a wheelchair and on my feet. I actually had to make friends leave the hospital, because they made me laugh so hard it hurt."

Fred was a liquor salesman from upper New York State. He frequently over-tested his products. Late one night, he wrapped his sports car around a tree, sustaining a lot of injuries, especially a badly cut-up face.

Fred managed to extricate himself from the remains of his car. He could see a light on in a farm house not too far away. He knocked on the door. A woman opened the door, saw Fred's cut-up face and looked horrified.

Fred quickly said, *"Trick or Treat!"*

Brian, "My wife, Sharon, insisted her nose was too big. I thought she looked great, but she wanted a nose job.

"When she woke up in recovery, Sharon was in a lot of pain. I asked if she needed anything.

"She said, 'Just get me a casket.'

"I said, *'Well, at least you can close the lid now.'*"

Kathy, "My brother had his legs and arms amputated because of diabetes. I started calling him my 'half-brother.' He loved it."

Intimacy
is created when we
LAUGH
through our fears
Together

Tom has been married to Diane for over 45 years. Tom is deaf and he just found out he has an eye disease that would make him go blind in about two months.

Tom laughed and said,

"Soon, my wife won't bother me at all. And the funniest part ... she agrees."

A common quote from caregivers: "Laughing keeps us from crying."

Erika, "I needed a kidney transplant. My loving husband gave me one of his. Now our song we sing together and dance to is,

"'I've got you under my skin.'"

Samantha, "Our dad had a series of strokes. We cared for him around the clock.

"Dad lives in the past most of the time and we learned to go along with him or we'd go nuts.

"One night my sister, Allison and I were both struggling to get dad on the toilet. After we got him seated he said, 'You both have it now, but I'm okay.'

"I asked who has what. He said, 'The Clap, you know gonorrhea.'

"The next night dad told me it was time to get ready to go. I asked where we were going. He said to Sue's wedding. Sue is another one of my sisters who lives out-of-town. She has been married for 40 years.

"When I told Allison what dad said about Sue she responded:

"'Oh great, Sue gets a wedding and we get gonorrhea.'"

Rich

"I called my pregnant wife. I barely got out, 'Hello,' before she said, 'Call back in 15 minutes. I'm expecting a call from the doctor,' and hung up.

"Fifteen minutes later I found out my adorable wife confused her prenatal pills with our dog, Elroy's, heartworm medication. She accidentally took the dog's pills and called the doctor to see if she or the baby were in danger. The doctor assured her they would both be fine.

"I asked if she gave Elroy the prenatal pills. She said,

"'What do you think I am, stupid?'

"I knew better to answer."

Kim

"I watched my father wither away in a 9-year battle with multiple myeloma. Every time he saw his primary care physician, he would ask, 'Do you have a cure yet?'

"Every time he heard, 'No, Ed, not yet,' he would smile and say, 'Well, what good are you then?' and laugh.

"My father loved to laugh. I firmly believe that is why his doctor's prognosis of 2 to 5 years was short by nearly 100%.

"Dad would constantly state, 'You can go through life's travels and obstacles angry, pissed off at the world or you can go happy finding the humor in all things.'

"'Since no one is going to get out of this life alive, why not enjoy the trip?'"

Chapter 4

TOUGH JOBS

The COURT JESTER

Remember the court jester? If he didn't make the king laugh, he got his head cut off. You are no different. If you don't make yourself laugh, you'll lose your head. And maybe your job.

The toughest part of any job is dealing with a boss, co-worker, or customer. People can be difficult and often times unpredictable. You have a choice: ignore them, deal with them, or do time in prison. The most effective way to handle conflict and get back to enjoying your work is HUMOR.

The following true stories show how real people found their inner-jester and laughed smack dab in a kaleidoscope of conflict. When faced with a problem, they didn't get mad or feel sorry for themselves. They kept their head, their job and they laughed.

You can do the same.

David

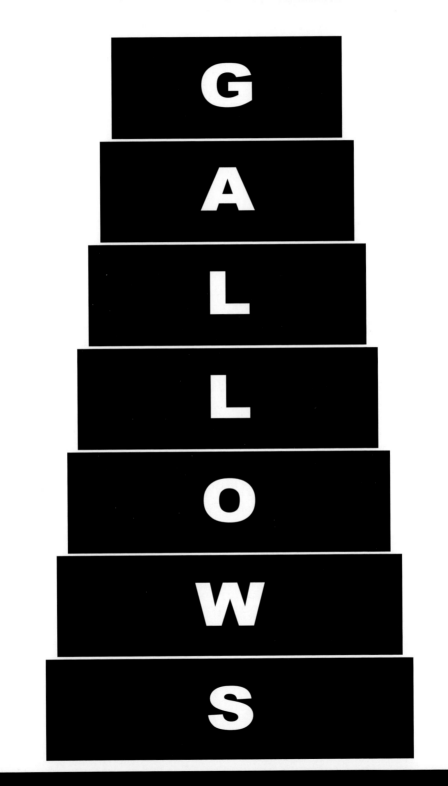

Gallows Humor is produced in Gallows situations. The humor created in a hopeless or desperate condition keeps the focus on survival. Gallows humor prevents emotions from paralyzing one's ability to get through the situation and DO THEIR JOB.

NO ONE is qualified to judge or condemn anyone's use of humor. Firefighters, First Responders, Military, Health Care Professionals, or anyone who offers a service in a life or death situation has a job to do. They cannot let emotions interfere with the services they provide and have been trained to give.

So, they find humor and laugh.

*"Humor is not a way to deny our feelings.
It is a way to navigate through them."*
– Paul Noberga, Retired Paramedic

*"An officer who stays in the career
learns to externalize rather than
internalize what they see and hear. And
you do that with humor and laughter."*
– John Raulerson, Retired Police Officer

Leo Hernandez
Deputy Sheriff for over 25 years.

"Autopsies are one of the more grisly aspects of my job. I recently attended one of a local gang member. He had been shot in the head by another gang member.

"The pathologist began his work while I photographed the procedure. They usually keep the cause of death simple like: 'stab wound to the chest' or 'trauma to the neck.'

"In this case I was fully expecting him to tell me cause of death would be gunshot to the head. Instead, he says,

"'Cause of death, failure to duck.'

"I paused for a moment, then saw a grin come across his face, followed by a giggle. Understand, this type of humor only happens between us. Inside jokes, while likely morbid to others, are one of the tools we use to maintain our humanity and to do our job in the best way."

Cops

LA Police lucked out with a robbery suspect. When detectives asked each man in the lineup to repeat the words: "Give me your money or I'll shoot."

One man shouted,
"That's not what I said!"

A retired police officer, "One steamy summer night, my partner and I saw a bleeding man crawling down a country road. The guy had been sprayed with buckshot. He wouldn't tell us where the shooting took place. We followed the blood trail to a house with a broken window.

"An old man answered the door. We asked if he heard any shooting.

"'Yep,' he said, 'I did it.'

"We asked him to explain.

"'I was in bed, half-asleep. Somebody broke my bedroom window. When he crawled through, I shot him.'

"We asked why he didn't call the police.

"'Didn't need to,' the old man said. *'I shot him back out.'*

"We arrested the burglar."

Policewoman Pat Rodgers

"It was the perfect setting for an interrogation – a dirty, old room with a single light bulb and a thunderstorm raging outside. One of our officers was intensely questioning a suspect.

"The officer got in the suspect's face and screamed, 'The Lord wants you to confess!'

"The instant the word 'confess' got out of the officer's mouth, a tremendous bolt of lightning struck the building. It scared us cops pretty good, but nothing like the suspect. He immediately confessed to everything – even stuff we didn't know about."

Pat continues, "I like to wear a necklace with a pig-shaped charm. It came in handy when I was called to break up a street brawl. One of the kids fighting saw my necklace and laughed.

"He yelled, 'Hey look. The pig is wearing a pig!' The kids walked over to see my pig charm. They laughed. The fight stopped."

In Bay City, Michigan, a woman was working the midnight shift at a convenience store. A man entered and wandered around for over 20 minutes. The clerk got frightened, worrying the man was going to rob her.

He approached, setting a can of pork and beans on the counter. Relieved, the clerk turned around to ring up the sale. When she turned back, the man had exposed himself – placing "it" on the counter.

She picked up the can of pork and beans and slammed it on his exposed organ. The guy dropped. Slamming his head on the counter, he flopped unconscious on the floor.

The clerk dialed 911 and the police arrived within minutes. The man was arrested once he regained consciousness.

Escorting him to the squad car, a policeman said,

"Bet you next time you'll try to buy a loaf of bread, won't you?"

NYC Police Officer Frank Montlione, "One afternoon during a heavy snowstorm, wacky old Mrs. Lighter reported a theft at her house. When I walked in she said, 'Those little monkeys are stealing my electricity again. They hide in the garage and run out to the meter.'

"I did everything I could not to laugh. She walked around the side of the house to show me the meter. I wanted to point out that our footprints were the only ones in the snow. No monkey prints. I didn't say anything. It would only have made her wackier.

"We went inside. I told her I would check for monkeys and left. I immediately called the station and thanked the guys for this assignment.

"Everyone at the station knew Mrs. Lighter. She called a lot. A typical call might go like this:

Mrs. L: 'The monkeys are here with ray guns.'
Me: 'What you need to do is wrap your legs in tinfoil to deflect the ray.'
Mrs. L: 'I did that last week. It didn't work. They're going to kill me.'
Me: 'Let me transfer you to homicide.'
Mrs. L: 'No, wait. It starts as a burning sensation in the legs.'
Me: 'Let me transfer you to arson.'
Mrs. L: 'Oh no, the little monkeys are back.'
Me: 'I'm sorry. We only handle big monkeys. The juvenile detectives handle the little ones.'
Mrs. L: 'The man I spoke to last week sent over a special unit to spy on the aliens. Could you send him back?'
Me: 'Sure. Look out the window. What color was the car that just went by?'
Mrs. L: 'Brown.'
Me: 'That's them.'
Mrs. L: 'My, they're fast.'

"She also told me the monkeys hijacked a satellite and were showing her life story without her authorization. They were actually not after her – they were only after her house. She never called again.

"I guess the monkeys got the house."

Ken, "Domestic disturbances are usually no fun, but my partner and I make them funny any chance we get.

"One time, we arrived at a scene where a couple was screaming and throwing things. They said they hated each other, wishing they had never married.

"I pulled out a police book and had them put their hands on it. Then I made up some legal double-talk, granting them a 'temporary divorce.' They actually believed it, so we left.

"Another night, we went to investigate a loud music complaint. The party people apologized, assuring us they would keep the sound down. Minutes later we were called back. The obnoxious drunks again apologized and promised to keep it down.

"After the third call, we knocked but no one would answer. My partner put a can of mace at the base of the door. He turned on the spray and said, *'This will shut them up. Let's go.'*

"*Another time,* we got a noise complaint from an apartment building known for loud, glue-sniffing parties. We questioned everybody at the party. Everyone denied any glue sniffing. They also stated they were not being loud.

"As my partner and I insisted, we could smell glue. Someone started screaming outside the apartment. We walked out of the apartment and looked down the hall. It was 'Crazy Alice.' Everybody knew Crazy Alice – a loud, obnoxious transvestite.

"'We're not hurting anybody,' Alice screamed. 'We're not doing anything wrong. Go away!'

"I told Alice we weren't leaving until the glue-sniffing stopped. Other neighbors started coming out of their apratments into the hall.

"Alice pulled out a knife and put it to her (or his) throat, and threatened to commit suicide if we didn't leave. All the neighbors started chanting,

"'Do it, Alice! Do it!'"

Officer Parker, "A fellow officer stopped four suspicious men in Apache Junction, Arizona. One was taken to jail for an outstanding warrant.

"The other three worked up a plan to get his bail money. They decided to rob a convenience store and couldn't have screwed it up more.

"They parked in front, in full view of the clerk. They showed their faces to the security camera. They demanded an amount of money equal to their friend's bail, and headed straight to the jailhouse.

"During the two-mile drive, the robbery and the robbers' physical descriptions had been reported to the police station.

"When the three crooks walked into the police station, the desk sergeant took the bail money. He escorted the men to where their buddy was being held and shut the door behind them."

A Police Officer in Irvine, Texas pulled over a woman for speeding. She was belligerent, insisting he should be out catching criminals instead of trapping speeders. She kept asking if he had some sort of daily quota.

"Yes Ma'am," the officer said. "With this ticket I'm giving you, I win a free toaster."

She didn't laugh. As a matter of fact, it turned out she was the mayor's wife. The woman complained to the chief of police.

The officer received a reprimand. A week later, however, the officer got a letter from the mayor praising the officer's sense of humor and encouraging him to continue using it in public. The mayor also apologized for his wife's lack of a sense of humor.

Enough

Bruno, "Christmas Eve, my partner and I were called to a house where an eight-month-old baby drowned in the tub. The mom had forgotten about her baby in the tub because she was getting drunk with her boyfriend.

"The next call was a 15-year-old girl who told us to arrest her father. Her dad had been molesting her for years. She called us because he said he was done with her. It was time to 'break in' her 11-year-old sister.

"The last call of the day we went to a trailer court. Two boys, eight and ten, were crying. They had been saving their paper route money to buy Christmas presents for their mom, a single parent, working three jobs.

Someone broke in
and stole all the gifts.

"After my shift, I went home and poured a drink. I was alone on Christmas Eve except for booze and a loaded revolver in my lap.

"I took a big drink. Thinking how horrible people can be, I picked up the gun. As I drew it closer to my head, the phone rang. I thought about ignoring the call. I considered shooting the damn phone.

"I answered. Another cop was calling to wish me Merry Christmas. She talked about her crazy day, laughing. Her stories got me giggling. She asked how I was. I told her I needed to talk and asked if I could come over. She said sure. I put the gun away and went to her house.

"The next day I turned in my badge. It was time for another line of work.

"Laughing literally saved my life."

In Vancouver, British Columbia, there is a bridge where suicidal people go to jump. One time an officer tried for six hours to stop a man from jumping. The man jumped anyway. Because the rescue team was already in place, the man was pulled from the water uninjured.

Imitating an Olympic judge, one of the cops wrote 5.0 on a piece of paper and held it up for a cop on the other side of the bridge to see. That cop wrote 5.5 and held it up in response.

All of the policemen got a great laugh, but a woman watching was irate, accusing the officers of being insensitive.

A policeman told her, "This is how we order coffee from a distance: 5.0 means black; 5.5 is for cream and sugar."

The woman believed him.

EMT, Chris Maltese, "In my job, you see some extremely grotesque and frightening things. If you don't make light of it, you'll end up in a padded room.

"Once, we were dispatched to a subway. A train hit a homeless man. His head was launched forward and his body ended up at the back of the train.

"This was my first decapitation. I was nervous. My EMT partner went up the tracks to find the head.

"He called me on the walkie-talkie and asked me to come up for assistance. When I got there, he was sitting next to the "head" singing a line from the old song, 'I'm Just a Gigolo.'

"'I ain't got no-body!'"

Teachers

Today, teachers are bombarded by disrespectful students, unappreciative parents and intimidating administrators. Humor is their well-deserved emotional release. Laughing is their most effective way to blow off the overwhelming stresses of their job.

David

Anne Jones was teaching her fourth graders about birds. Ryan raised his hand and asked, "Where do birds go to the bathroom?"

The class laughed. Ms. Jones wasn't sure how to answer. She didn't have to think long. A girl in the back row said, "Anywhere they want."

Another afternoon, Ms. Jones was teaching plant reproduction. She started with, "Plants are different from animals. Animals must mate to reproduce."

Allen raised his hand and asked, "Ms. Jones, what does 'mate' mean?"

The teacher was prepared. She knew exactly what to say. But then she saw another student whispering something in Allen's ear. He listened intently and wrinkled his forehead. Then he slowly nodded and said, "Ohhhh, I get it.'

Ms. Jones smiled and continued on with her lesson on plant reproduction.

Elementary

Margaret Kelly is a third-grade music teacher. Each year, she has her students write an essay on famous composers. Here are some of her favorite excerpts.

MOZART
Mozart was born and died at age 35.
He composed music for small pianos.
Mozart's mother died in Paris and that's why his music sounds Italian. He died of an illness and then he was poor and lonesome.

BACH
Bach wanted to write church music, but he got married instead. His mother and father died at the age of 10. Bach was a devout Lutheran, but he also believed in God

GERSHWIN
Gershwin wrote songs at 15, but learned about composition later. He was good at the technical stuff he learned while working on his knuckles. Gershwin wrote Un-American in Paris.

BEETHOVEN
Beethoven caught a serious cold at the end of 1826 and died for a year. Beethoven was half-German, half-English, and half-Italian. His death was the reason he quit composing.

Middle School

Ms. Britton, "I don't send students who swear to the principal's office. It's not much of a punishment. Instead, I use a 'cuss bucket.' A swear word costs $1.00; the f-word is $5.00. The money goes to charity.

"One day, a student named Luke was messing around in class. He yelled out, 'Damn.'

"I told him to put a dollar in the bucket. Luke protested, arguing that 'damn' is said on television all the time.

"'True,' I said. 'They also have sex on television, but I don't want you doing that in my classroom either.'

"The students went crazy. Luke laughed and put four quarters in the bucket."

A student was trying to stir up trouble. He didn't like what the teacher had assigned and said to the class, "Let's refuse. Let's have a sit-in or go on strike. Come on, who's with me? Where are my supporters?"

No one answered.

"Apparently," the teacher said, "the only supporter you have is in your gym bag."

The students loved it. No more attempts to stir up trouble from that young man.

High School

A high school English teacher was reminding her class of the next day's final. She told her class there would be no excuses for missing the test, except for injury, illness or a death in the family. A male student, known for frequent disruptions, asked,

"What about sexual exhaustion?"

The class burst into laughter. The teacher patiently waited for the laughter to stop, then smiled and said, "I guess you'll have to write with your other hand, won't you?"

Christina Foster is a high school guidance counselor. Over the years she has saved dozens of notes written by parents to excuse a child's absence.

"Please excuse Joe. He has loose vowels."

"My son is under the doctor's care and should not take P.E. class. Please execute."

"Please excuse Joyce from Jim. She is administrating."

"Please ackuse John been absent of January 28, 29, 30, 22 and 33. John has been absent from school because he had two teeth taken out of his face."

"Please excuse Gloria. She had been sick and under the doctor."

"Please excuse Blanch from P.E. for a few days. She fell out of a tree and misplaced her hip."

"Please excuse Diane from being absent yesterday. She is in bed with gramps."

Tom is a high-school teacher in an affluent area. He has to put up with the tantrums and antics of spoiled teenagers.

Tom, "A student came in with a flamboyant new 'Mohawk' hairstyle. I attempted to pay him a compliment saying, 'That is some new haircut.'

"The boy didn't react the way I hoped. Instead, he got mad and said, 'Why are you making fun of my hair? Why is it such a big deal? Do you have a problem with it?'

"I said, 'No, I don't. I was actually giving you a compliment. But since you are choosing to be negative, your hair looks like it's held up by axle grease.'

"The other students laughed.

"'Mohawk Boy' stormed out of the room with his backpack in one hand, and flipped me off with the other.

"Three weeks later, I was handing out grade cards. 'Mohawk Boy' got his and screamed, 'Hey! I got a 79 and you gave me a "C." That's not fair! A "B" is only 80 points.' He kept making a scene.

"Very calmly, I looked at him and said with a smile, 'That's right; 79 is a "C."' Then I held up my middle finger, and said smiling,

"'And only one point away from a "B."'"

Rags, "Several of my high school students are on probation. They are court-ordered to stay in school. These kids don't respond to the threat of parental or administrative notification. Mention their probation officer, though, and they straighten right up.

"One student, Donny, was causing so much trouble, it was time for the probation officer threat. Coincidentally, I noticed Donny's probation officer standing in the hall. I casually walked toward the door and motioned him in. Donny was shocked.

"I said, 'Donny your officer and I have a psychic connection. All I have to do is think about him and he'll show up.'

"Donny believed it. His behavior and grades dramatically improved.

L auren Hofteig, "Growing up, I had no problem getting into trouble. Once in fifth grade, for some unknown reason, I decided to trip my teacher, Miss Splettstazer. She was a very big lady. When I stuck out my ankle, she went down hard.

"What surprised me was the speed with which she got up, grabbed my right ear and yanked me from my seat. She pulled me backwards down the aisle and out the classroom door. I was towed through the hall, down the steps to the main floor. While my ear and body made the trip with Miss Splettstazer, my feet were always three steps behind.

"I was thrown into a chair directly in front of the principal's desk. Principal Evelyn Crarey was a 4' 10" bowling ball with feet. She went to a wooden cabinet to find my file, repeating 'Hofteig, Lauren, Hofteig, Lauren …' as she went through the drawer. She found my file then sat at her desk, 'Well, Hofteig, Lauren.'

"'Yes, Crarey, Evelyn?' I said.

"That caught her by surprise. A smile flashed across her face, but that didn't stop her from calling my mother.

"When I got home from school, mom sat me in my bedroom and told to stay there until my father got home.

"When dad walked in he was greeted with, 'Guess what Lauren did today?' Not one detail was left out. Dad sat in his chair, looked at me and said, 'I understand we got a phone call from school today.'

"'Yes, sir,' I said.

"'What should we do about that?' he asked.

"'Disconnect the phone?' I asked.

"That caught dad off-guard. He smiled. Then laughed. He kept laughing for a good two minutes. He was so tickled, he didn't punish me. I couldn't believe it. I got off scott-free.

"Mom was so mad she didn't speak to him for two weeks."

Teaching Humorously

Mr. Wheeler begins, "People can learn more when it's presented humorously.

"In my 45 years of teaching, I was called to the principal's office many times for my use of humor. I would tell my senior high-school students every year, 'I want some of you to fail because when I lower the electric windows on my car – going through the drive-thru, I need someone to serve me fries.'

"One year I was called to the principal's office with an angry father. After the dad told the drive-thru story and how he was offended, the principal said, 'Mr. Wheeler tells his students that story every year to wake them up – to inspire them to continue their education.'

"I stopped the dad after the meeting and said, 'Your son is doing nothing in class. He doesn't participate and doesn't do his homework. If he keeps that up, one of the only places he will be working is fast-food.'

"It worked. The boy's grade went from an F to an A. He also finished the year with Straight 'A's' in all of his classes."

The Light Goes on ...

Bill, "I taught a first-semester graduate course in clinical interviewing. One lesson was recognizing suicide risk. If someone is showing high-risk signs such as depression and hopelessness, one must find out if they are considering suicide. I instructed the students to ask directly, in a matter-of-fact way.

"Towards the end of the year, I supervised (via one-way mirror) clinical students conducting their first intake interview. A student named Lloyd was interviewing a man who showed classic risk signs. The man was slumped forward in his chair, mostly staring at the floor, his face full of pain and defeat.

"He said, 'I'm worthless at work, no good to my family. I have no real friends. Sometimes I just don't think it's worth it.'

"Behind the mirror I'm thinking, 'Come on, Lloyd, remember what I told you!'

"Then I saw the light go on in his eyes. Lloyd leaned forward, looked the client right in the eye, and asked,

"'Well, have you considered suicide?"

SPORTS

College basketball coach Jimmy Valvano constantly argued with officials. During one game, Valvano got hit with a technical foul.

He was warned to keep his mouth shut or be kicked out of the game. The coach suffered through several more of what he considered bad calls. During a time-out, Valvano asked the official, "Can I get kicked out for what I'm thinking?"

The ref said he couldn't.

Jimmy V shot back, "I think your officiating sucks."

Valvano got another technical but wasn't kicked out of the game.

The referee was laughing too hard.

Floyd Little was an All-American running back at Syracuse University. He went on to become an All-Pro in the NFL

Floyd, "As a running back, you could never let the opposing team know they hurt you. Dick Butkus of the Chicago Bears was one of the hardest hitting linebackers in NFL history. One time, Butkus tackled me so hard, I didn't think there were any fluids left in my body.

"I didn't want to let him know how bad he shook me up, so I got up and said, 'Is that all you got? Was that your best hit?'

"Butkus looked at me and said, 'You okay, Floyd?'

"I said, 'I thought you were a hard hitter, man.'

"Butkus asked again if I was okay. I finally said, 'Why do you keep asking me that?'

"'Because you're in the wrong huddle, Floyd.'"

The Chinook Sugar Bears were challenging the Browning Indians in a high school basketball game.

Dr. Kent Hjelmstad, "I was refereeing. Browning's coach was being obnoxious. He was yelling and screaming way too much. When I called a traveling foul on Browning, he ran on the court and started yelling. Running on the court after a ref makes a call is a major violation.

"I blew the whistle. My patience had run out. I told him that every step back to his seat would cost him a technical foul.

"The coach summoned two of his players and said, 'Carry me back to the bench.'

"I wasn't expecting that. Sure enough, they carried him all the way to his seat. He looked at me with a big grin and I started laughing.

"The crowd loved it. I can tell you this: He didn't scream any more."

Dara Torres was the first American swimmer to earn medals at three consecutive Olympics: 1984,1988 and 1992. Dara recalls the events leading up to the 400m freestyle final at Barcelona in 1992.

Dara, "Before the race, all the competitors gathered in a waiting room. The girls were sitting there, staring straight ahead or at each other – trying to be intimidating. I walked in with my headphones blasting and cheerfully shouted, 'What's up everybody!' Nobody reacted.

"At the pool, I jumped right in and splashed around to get used to the temperature. Since I was the only one in the pool, all the other swimmers glared at me. Just for fun, I spit water into their lanes, like a fountain. Because I laughed and was silly, I relaxed. I guess it worked. I took the gold."

Mike Eruzione, "We had tied Sweden and unexpectedly defeated the Czech Republic. Our third game was against Norway. After the first period, we were down by one goal. Coach Brooks stormed into the locker room and screamed,

"'What are you doing? You're not playing as a team. When you play as a team you can beat anybody. You have to work together and talk to each other. If someone makes a great defensive play, tell him. If someone makes a save, tell him. Compliment each other. Play as a team!' He stormed out.

"The locker room was silent for 30 seconds. Eric Strobel looks to Dave Silk and says, 'I love the way you wear your hair.' Everyone laughed. That's exactly what we needed to calm our nerves. We defeated Norway and went on to beat Romania and West Germany.

"We were set to play Russia.

"No one ever expected us to come this far. The locker room was quiet. Our locker room was never quiet. There was always some guy doing something crazy. Today was different.

"Coach Brooks walks in and quietly says, 'You were born to be a player. You were meant to be here. This moment is yours.' And he walked out.

"I had no idea what the heck he was talking about. Neither did anybody else. The silence was broken when Davey Christian stood and said, 'I am going to be flying tonight.' He had a pair of wings taped to his helmet.

"That busted up our nervous tension. We went out and beat the Russians. In 1980 the United States Olympic Hockey Team was, maybe, going to take 7th place. No one ever expected us to win the gold."

Bill Veck was legendary in the baseball world for his wacky promotions and his gift of gab.

One summer night, while World War 2 was raging overseas, Bill stood on top of the Wisconsin Hotel. Merv Connors, first baseman for Veck's hapless Chicago Cubs, was drunk on the ledge and threatening to jump.

Cautiously, Veck asked, "Merv, have I ever been unfair to you?"

"There's one thing I got to say for you Bill," Connors said, staring at the pavement. "You've treated me well."

"Then I'm entitled to ask you for a small favor?" Veck asked gently.

Merv glared, certain Veck would try to talk him out of jumping.

Veck continued, anticipating Merv's suspicions.

"Merv, I'd be the last guy to stop you from doing what you want. But could you wait until I call the newspaper so they can get a picture of you hitting the sidewalk? You'd make every front page in the country. And you have to admit, Merv, the team could use the publicity. Maybe you could change into your uniform first?"

Connors laughed. Then, without a word, he climbed off the ledge, got in bed fully clothed and passed out. They never spoke of the incident again.

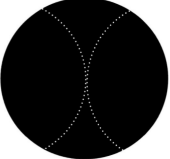

Ernie, "Pain has always been my friend. I've had broken ribs, a cracked sternum and have broken my nose seven times. My knees were twisted like pretzels. I crushed the carpal tunnel bones in both hands.

"One game, I broke my thumb. With blood all over my uniform, I stuck the bone back in, walked to the huddle, and casually asked,' What's the defense for this play?'

"Before a game against the Cleveland Browns, I was mistakenly given Demerol instead of Novocaine – 1,200 milligrams – enough to knock out a horse.

"Four hours later, I couldn't tell if I was awake or dreaming. A nurse was holding an oxygen mask over my mouth shouting, 'Breathe, damn it, breathe!'

"My eyes opened. One of the doctors asked me, 'Do you know who you are?'

"'Yeah, I think I'm Ernie Stautner.'

"'Do you know what you were supposed to do today?'

"'I was supposed to beat the Browns. But somehow, Doc, I don't think I made it.'

"I saw him go over to a group of physicians. They were whispering. I was sure something was wrong.

"'Give me a priest,' I shouted, then fell asleep. A nurse yelled,

"'Breathe, damn it, breathe!'

"A priest arrived and said to me, 'Do you think you are going to die?'

"'Yes, father. I need to say my last confession. Father bless me, for I have sinned ...'

"I stopped. I was feeling dizzy. The room was starting to move and getting darker.

"'Excuse me father', I continued, 'I don't have much time. Is it all right if I just ...

Hit the highlights?'"

Tim Brooks, "The emotional challenge of being a hospital chaplain runs in extremes. One moment, I'm celebrating the birth of a baby; the next, I am facing a pediatric death. I'd better keep my sense of humor.

"Once, I was called to the oncology unit. A 50-year-old patient was throwing a fit; hurling insults and objects.

"I walked in and said, 'Hi, I'm Chaplain Brooks. I wanted to meet you.'

"The patient glared and snarled, 'Well, you've met me. Now what?'

"'How are things going?' I calmly asked.

"'What am I supposed to do,' she snapped, 'take out my halo and put on my sanctimonious face?'

"'Sure,' I said, 'if that will make you feel better, please do.'

"She threw a couple more snide comments. I kept my replies pleasant and non-confrontational.

"When she realized I wouldn't run away, her demeanor changed. She began to open up and share her fear. She told me she had a mastectomy a year ago and now had lumps in her other breast.

"'No wonder you're afraid,' I said.

"'I sure am,' she said. 'Pray with me.'

"I took her hand and began to pray out loud.

"Then I realized I didn't know the woman's name. I tried to get out of it by using a lot of 'hers' and 'shes.' She squeezed my hand and whispered to please say my name.'

"'Okay,' I said, not knowing what to do.

"'It's Shirley.'

"'Thank you.'

"We prayed for a few minutes more. As I was leaving, she said, 'Don't forget to visit while I'm here. And bring a dirty joke to tell.'"

Bill Mahoney found out he had cancer of the bone, liver, pancreas, arms, head, legs and back.

"I got cancer every place but my lungs," he said.

"I'm sure glad I didn't quit smoking."

Diane Strudwick, "I worked at a hospital where a very troubled patient jumped from the roof and died. That was not funny.

"A few hours later, a nurse pointed out that the man landed in front of a sign which read: *'Patient Drop Off.'*"

You know you're a nurse if ...

... Standing in line at the grocery store, you find yourself checking out other customers' veins.

... You'd like to meet the inventor of the call light in a dark alley.

... The stories you tell in restaurants make people at other tables sick.

... You now use more four-lettered words than you even knew before.

... Every time someone asks for a pen, you find at least six on you.

... To be right is only half the battle. Convincing a doctor is more difficult.

... Your bladder gets to the size of a Winnebago.

... On your day off, you avoid unhealthy looking people for fear they'll drop and you'll have to do CPR.

... You have seen more penises than a prostitute.

You have to share the funny.

Bob Martin manages a retirement facility. To create a better working environment, Bob holds special weekly meetings where the staff shares the funny things that happen on the job.

At one such meeting, a nurse named Susan told a story about two residents having an intimate relationship. Susan was concerned because the 78 year-old woman was beginning to suffer from Alzheimer's. Susan decided to talk to the woman's 81-year-old boyfriend.

Susan told the gentleman that he had to end the intimate aspect of their relationship. He insisted he was doing nothing against her will.

Then she told him, 'You have to understand, she has Alzheimer's. She doesn't know what she is doing.'

"The hell she doesn't, he said."

When Bob took over managing the facility he noticed there were cans of brightly colored paints in the back store room. Since the retirement center was drab, he immediately had his staff repaint every room. He made sure everyone participated in the project.

Bob, "It changed everyone's attitude – including our residents. People were in a better mood and were happier. You know that paint is like humor ...

It's only good if you use it.

Joanne is a flight attendant for Southwest Airlines. She makes sure passengers pay attention to her safety speech by making them laugh.

"Ladies and gentlemen, if you could please give your attention to the other flight attendants, who include my husband Dave and his ex-wife Susan, they'd like to point out the safety features of the aircraft.

"For those of you who haven't been in an automobile lately and used your seat belt, slide the flat end into the buckle. Tying the belts together is not acceptable.

"I know they've told you there are 50 ways to leave your lover. We have only six ways on this aircraft – two forward doors, two over-the-wing exits and two aft.

"We certainly don't anticipate a change in the cabin pressure, but should one occur, four margarine cups will magically appear overhead. When they do, stop screaming, place the cup over your nose and mouth and breathe normally until notified by crew members or until Susan comes by offering mouth-to-mouth to all who need or want it.

"There's no smoking at all on board this aircraft. We prohibit smoking in the lavatories and if we find you doing so, Dave will ask you to step out on the wing, where you can also enjoy our patio furniture and the movie, 'Gone With the Wind.'

"Enjoy your flight. If there's anything else you need during this flight, call on Dave. Susan and I will be in the back, finishing our nails."

When the plane landed ...

"On behalf of Southwest Airlines we'd like thank you. Do us one last favor, keep your tush to the cush, your seat belt fastened and the luggage right where it is until Captain America and Boy Wonder pull this aircraft up to the gate and turn off the fasten seat belt signs. That will be your only indication that it's safe to jump up, grab all your luggage and go absolutely nowhere!

"We have a special gentleman on board today celebrating his 98th birthday and his first flight. Do me a big favor and wish our captain a Happy Birthday on your way out."

Military

Billy, "In Vietnam, one of my buddies got his leg blown off during combat. As we put him on the medical helicopter, he said, 'Now I can go home and kick some prosthetic 'ass.'"

Decorated Vietnam vet

Steve Caruso, "We lived on one canteen of water and one can of C-Rations per day. With poor sanitary conditions and hot, miserable weather, vomiting and diarrhea were an everyday occurrence.

"Our food had to be dropped by helicopter. One time, thanks to a typical military mistake, we got nothing but cases of plums. We were so sick of C-Rations, we ate them by the handful.

"Man, if you thought we had a diarrhea problem before, triple it. What made it worse was we could only relieve ourselves at night. Enemy scouts watched all day for any movement – no pun intended. If they saw anything move, they launched artillery. We had to hold it all day long then sneak off at night. There wasn't enough darkness. To make it worse, we ran out of toilet paper. We had to order an emergency supply. The helicopter dumped the paper in a field of ten-foot-high elephant grass. It took 50 guys to find it.

"The biggest cheer of my entire Vietnam duty came when that toilet paper was triumphantly paraded into camp. You would have thought we won the war."

Humorous Military Quotes

"Aim toward the Enemy."
– Instructions on U.S. Rocket
Launcher

*"When the pin is pulled,
Mr. Grenade is not our friend."*
– U.S. Marine Corps

*"You, you and you ... panic.
The rest of you, come with me!"*
– Marine Corps Sgt.

*"Never tell the platoon sergeant you
have nothing to do."*
– Marine Recruit

*"If you see a bomb technician
running, follow him."*
– USAF Ammo Troop

*"You've never been lost until you've
been lost at Mach 3."*
– Paul Crickmore, Test Pilot

*"The only time you have too much
fuel is when you're on fire."*
– USAF Trainer

USN. Captain Duffy Hutton

Duffy, "In July of 1965, I was assigned to the USS VAH-I, which stopped at Subic Bay on its way to Vietnam. While there, I ordered a personalized belt buckle. It was to be engraved with my name and squadron. I was told the buckle would not be ready before my unit left for Vietnam, so I planned to pick it up on the way home. I was shot down in October of 1965 and captured.

"Some time later, Red McDaniel and his unit passed through Subic on their way to Vietnam. An officer who knew me saw my finished belt buckle in the shop and told Red that I was a POW.

"Five years later, Red was also captured during combat. He joined our group at the Hanoi Hilton. I received a tap message on my wall from Red. The message was, 'Duffy, your belt buckle is ready to be picked up at Subic.'

"That's the funny stuff that kept me going."

"I was working on a submarine. One of the watch standers fell asleep on a step in the engine room. Remember, it's over 100 degrees down there.

"The lower-level watch climbed up behind him and tied a hose with a slipknot pointing at his 'plumber's pants' area and then dropped it back down to a lower level.

"A few seconds later, the hose jerked once and 35-degree water came squirting into his butt crack. He never fell asleep on that watch again.

"Another time, I was in charge of the diesel engine. We were on patrol when the front end overheated and we had to do an emergency shut down of the engine.

"I had just come off a 6-hour shift and was tired. It didn't matter. I had to fix that engine. The entire crew was counting on me.

"As I worked, a number of people kept coming up asking how it was coming along. I had gotten to the point where I was fed up with the interruptions. I was tired, working in a very confined space and it was extremely hot.

"Another person came up and asked me how it was going. I snapped back with, 'I would be doing a lot better and be a lot further along if everyone would stop bugging me.'

"I looked up. It was our Company Commander. Then, I finished my comment with, 'Sir.'

"He smiled and said, 'Nobody else will bother you. Please fix the problem as efficiently and quickly as you can.'

"'Thank you sir,' I instantly replied.

"Thank goodness he walked off laughing."

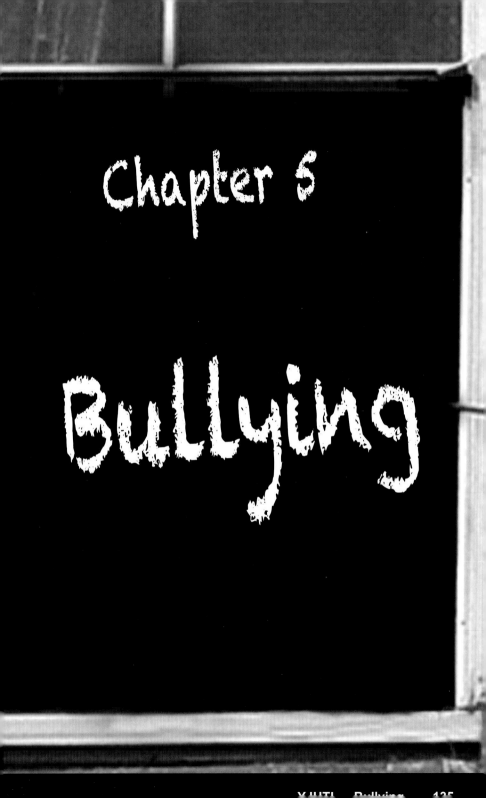

Chapter 5

Bullying

Why are people mean and rude?

Human Nature

How can we stop that behavior?

No One Can

Only mean and rude people can stop their own behavior.

You
can

STOP

someone
from
Bullying
YOU

First, let's get our terms accurate:

BULLYING
Using strength or power to harm or intimidate those who are weaker.

INSULT
Speak to or treat others
with disrespect or scornful abuse.

TEASE
Make fun or attempt to provoke in a playful or unkindly way.

SARCASM
To mock, meaning the opposite
of what is said. From the Greek word
"sarkazeint" – to tear flesh.

The VERBAL ATTACK

TEASING

A 5'3" man is on a elevator. A 6'6" tall man walks in. The shorter man says to the taller man, "I bet you played a lot of basketball when you were a kid."

INSULTING

A woman orders a bagel in a bakery. The man behind her says, "You don't need a bagel, you're fat enough."

SARCASM

A flight attendant is making coffee in the first-class compartment. A man walks by, sees her short, spiky hair and says to the guy in front of him, "Oh that hair looks good on her."

The COMEBACK

A humorous response to someone who teases, insults or is sarcastic.

Tall man says, "Yeah and I bet you played a lot of miniature golf when you were a kid."

Woman, "Is that what it is? I thought I was pregnant for all of these years."

Delivering the coffee the flight attendant said, "You know I think my hair is coming in quite good after chemo." (She wasn't doing chemo.)

WIT

* *keen intelligence*
* *mental sharpness*
* *using words and ideas in a quick and inventive way to create humor.*

The secret ...

to developing wit is to pay close attention to the insulter's words.

1. It keeps you from getting emotional. (Fear, anger and sadness kill funny thinking.)

2. Those insulter's words will be your ammunition for your comeback. When you turn around the words that were intended to hurt you, it shows that YOU are funnier, quicker and smarter than the insulter.

USE IT

Don't just think of clever comeback – use it. Too often, people think of a great comeback but are afraid to say it. Bouncing back an insulter's words keeps you from internalizing any negative energy.
And that insulter will think twice before bothering you again.

Bullying

The bully's intention is to harm using strength or power. Intimidation over someone weaker, is the bully's motivation.

The same comeback principles apply to the verbal bully. Just be aware when it's time to walk or run away, if it gets to the physical level. What makes a bully different is that they are usually looking for a fight - verbally or physically. You can choose to physically fight. Many times that stops a bully, too - but it can be dangerous.

We at aYJHTL are not suggesting you get in a physical fight with someone, but we have heard of stories where that is an effective way to stop a bully. We are solely offering suggestions in the verbal form of bullying to build self-esteem and wit.

David

Enter the BULLY

An airline cancelled a flight. The ticket counter agent had to handle a long line of irritated people by herself. A middle-aged man pushed his way to the front of the line, slapped his ticket on the counter and yelled, "I demand to be on the next flight – and it better be First Class!"

The agent said politely, "I'm sorry sir, I'll be happy to help, but these folks were in line first. As soon as I take care of them, I'll be glad to help you."

The man yelled back loud enough for everybody to hear, "Do you know who I am?"

The ticket agent took the microphone and calmly announced:

"Attention, please. We have a lost man. He doesn't know who he is. If anyone can identify him, please come to the counter."

The people in line laughed.

The man gritted his teeth. "Screw you lady!" he said.

"I'm sorry sir, but you'll have to wait in line for that, too," she replied.

Bullying is a self-esteem and parenting issue. A child learns at home how to deal with a bully. Whether to stand up to them or slither off into the cosmic sewer of low self-esteem. They learn both at home.

David

Way to Go Mom!

Amother begins, "My nine-year-old son was being called a 'fag' by a group of boys at school. He came home crying. I asked if he knew what 'fag' meant and he did.

"My son and I sat down with a dictionary. I had him write ten acronyms for 'fag.' We rehearsed and the boy was prepared and ready.

"The next day, the boys called him a 'fag' again. My son said, 'What?' And they repeated,

'You're a fag.'

"'Do you mean 'fun and great' or 'famous and goofy'? If you mean fabulous and grandiose, then, you're right. I'm a 'fag.'

"The boys were stunned. My son walked off smiling. Then the lead bully said, You're 'gay', too. My son turned and said with a smile, 'Do you mean 'giddy and yippidy' or 'gregarious and yurking.' The bullies were speechless.

"They never bothered him again. And my son feels great at how stood up to them."

Tara was 9 years old and in the 4th grade. She knew she was adopted and felt secure and happy with her now mother and father.

Some of the girls in her class found out she was adopted. One day the teacher left the class for a few minutes. Some of the girls gathered around Tara's desk and began bullying her. The reason it would be called bullying is that they were trying to harm and intimidate her as a group.

One of the girls said, "You're really adopted. Your real parents gave you away."

Another girl said, "They didn't even love you enough to keep you."

Tara stood up. She looked at the two girls who just made those rude comments and said,

"No, my mom and dad chose me and love me. Your parents got what they got."

A flight attendant brought down the great Muhammad Ali. At the height of his boxing career, the champ was flying to a fight. As the jet prepared for take off, the attendant told Ali to fasten his seat belt.

Ali said with a big grin, "Superman don't need a seat belt."

The flight attendant said with a bigger smile. "No sir, Superman doesn't need an airplane. You need to buckle your seatbelt.

Ali laughed and fastened his belt.

Musician Stevie Wonder was asked
if being blind hurt his career.
"It could have been tougher," Stevie said,
"I could have been black."

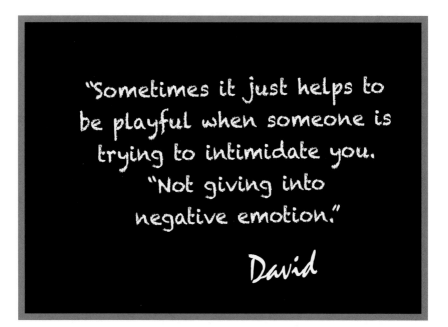

"Sometimes it just helps to
be playful when someone is
trying to intimidate you.
"Not giving into
negative emotion."

David

A plane left the gate at the Sky Harbor Airport. Ten minutes later a man came running through the terminal, screaming, "Hold that plane!"

He skidded to a halt at the ticket counter and yelled, "Where's the plane?"

The agent said calmly, "Which one?"

The man pointed to where the plane had been and said, "That one!"

"I'm sorry sir," she said, "that plane is gone."

"Where was it headed?"

"Los Angeles."

"Did it leave on time?"

"Yes."

"Call the plane."

"Why?"

"Tell the pilot to bring the plane back."

She picked up the phone and acted like she was talking to the pilot.

"Captain? Where are you? Oh, you're in the air. Can you come back, there's a man here who really needs to be on that plane. Oh, you can't."

She put her hand over the phone and asked the angry customer, "What should I do now?"

The man stood for a second then grinned.

"Tell him to go on," he said.

The agent booked the man on the next flight. He walked away smiling.

More Funny Comebacks

After every flight, Qantas Airline pilots fill out a form called a gripe sheet. Gripe sheets notify mechanics about any problems with the just-flown aircraft. The mechanics correct the problems and document the repairs. The pilots review the gripe sheet before the next flight.

Pilot: Something loose in cockpit.
Mechanic: Something tightened in cockpit.

P: Left inside main tire almost needs replacing.
M: Almost replaced left inside main tire.

P: Dead bugs on windshield.
M: Live bugs on back-order.

P: Evidence of leak on main landing gear.
M: Evidence removed.

P: DME volume unbelievably loud.
M: DME volume set to more believable level.

P: Friction locks cause throttle levers to stick.
M: That's what they're for.

P: Aircraft handles funny.
M: Aircraft warned to straighten up, fly right, and be serious.

P: Target radar hums.
M: Reprogrammed target radar with lyrics.

P. Noise coming from under instrument panel. Sounds like a midget pounding on something with a hammer.
M: Took hammer away from midget.

Mr. Leaf is a high school English teacher and Varsity Head Football Coach.

Mr. Leaf, "The first day of school I walked into my third-hour English class. When I walked to my desk and put down my briefcase, I heard the students giggling. I looked at them and they tried to hide their smirks. When I looked at the chalkboard, I saw what they were laughing about. It read,

"'Mr. Leaf eats SHIT.'

"I immediately grabbed a piece of chalk and wrote underneath it,
"'On rye toast.'
"I put the chalk back in the tray, turned around, smiled and stated, 'If you are going to write about me, you need to make sure it's accurate.'"

Ms. Clarkson is a middle school English teacher. Melissa was a 13-year-old who would constantly disrupt class with her vocal and inappropriate outbursts. It was obvious to the teacher that she was doing this to get attention.

One day Ms. Clarkson told Melissa,

"Control your mouth or I will send you to the principal."

Melissa shouted, "You're a whore."

Ms. Clarkson said, "What I do in my personal time is nobody's business."

The students went crazy laughing. Melissa never had any outbursts again. In fact, she turned into a very cooperative, good student - and a pleaure to have in class.

Best Laugh I ever got

Norm Alden, "After one of my late-night comedy shows, I took a waitress friend to her home. She was too drunk to drive.

"At her request, I dropped her off a block from her house. She claimed her husband was a light sleeper and the car noise would wake him up.

"The next afternoon, I was taking a nap outside in a lawn chair. When I woke up, I was staring down the barrel of a shotgun.

"The man holding the gun shouted, 'I know you were with my wife last night! I saw you drop her off! I wondered why she had been coming home late! Now I know!'

"Keeping cool I said, 'Take it easy. I gave your wife a ride home because she was too drunk to drive.'

"He didn't believe me and made up a story

"'I know you've been sleeping with her,' he continued, 'so now I am going to kill everybody! I am going to start with you, then her. Then I am going to finish myself off last!'

"I said, 'Well, that sounds like a plan. But why don't you start with yourself?'

"The husband kept glaring like he hadn't heard a word. Then, he slowly realized what I said and lowered the gun. He laughed. Best laugh I ever got. Then we went out and had a beer."

A senior in high school and his mom moved to Northern California. At his new high school, some of his classmates would cough the word "Jew" while passing in the halls. One bully regularly hit him in gym class.

Mom and he came up with an idea. Rather than tell school administrators about the bully, he would make a movie about him with his new camera.

He filmed the senior-class excursion. While shooting, he asked several students – including the bully and his buddies – to look up and flinch. When the film was shown at graduation, there was a scene of sea gulls flying. He had spliced in shots of the bully and his friends. It looked like they were being splattered on by the birds.

After the movie, the bully told the young filmmaker that he liked the film. He even apologized for his bad behavior and said he wished that he would have gotten to know him better.

That young filmmaker - Steven Spielberg.

Finding the funny in everything

Ms. Anonymous, "I like to make people laugh. I've been able to find the funny in almost every situation except with my dad. He is an extremely negative and angry man. I, on the other hand, am a happy adult in my mid twenties. I live very far away from him now, so his anger doesn't get to me any more.

"It was hard to be joyful growing up with such an angry man. Then one day it hit me – instead of fighting with my dad, I would 'outwit' him and find the funny.

"One time we were on vacation and he got very angry. I said, 'Dad relax! We are on vacation. Smile. Have some fun!'

"He snarled, 'Have some fun? Is that all life is about to you? FUN?' My immediate reaction was to get upset and fight back at him. Instead I laughed and said, 'I do like to have fun. And it's important to laugh in life.'

"He got even more angry and yelled, 'Yep, that's it, life is one big joke to you isn't it? You can never take anything seriously.'

"'Dad,' I said, 'I take my life very seriously, but I also like to have fun with it!'

"He's never going to change and find the funny at 67 years old, but I can!

"When we laugh at bullies' mean comments, and when we don't react to their anger they have no idea what to do. More people should do this."

Chapter 6

Dangerous Situations

Managing
FEAR

Bringing humor into a dangerous situation keeps us from being paralyzed by fear. And yet, fear can be a positive emotion because it protects.

When we recognize what we are afraid of and find humor, we become superior to the fear. Only then, can we begin to manage our fears.

David

Richie, a comedian, finished a late-night comedy set in midtown New York City. He had another show in Greenwich Village. A cab would cost him nearly all the money he just made. So, even though it can be dangerous that time of night, the comic took the subway.

He was relieved to find he was the only passenger in his car. That feeling didn't last. Six punk rockers came barging in, laughing and making a lot of noise with their military boots. They wore torn clothing and had multicolored Mohawks. Their faces were pierced like pin cushions.

All carried baseball bats.

The train started moving. The punkers started banging their bats on the floor, seats and windows. When they saw the comedian in the corner, they stopped. They stared at him. The comic broke the silence.

"Big game tonight, fellas?"

They joked all the way downtown.

Bob "Woodsy" Woods, a New York comic, had fallen on hard times. He was living in his car. After an evening performance, Woodsy got a ride "home" from his friend, Vinnie.

The temperature was near zero. Vinnie begged Woodsy not to sleep in his car, fearing he would freeze to death. Woodsy said he would be fine.

Vinnie pulled up to the car, pleading with his friend not to risk freezing to death. Woodsy said good night, thanked him for the ride, and went into the frigid night.

Vinnie, "As I drove off, I looked in my rear-view mirror and saw Woodsy frantically waving his arms. He was signaling me to come back. I hoped he was finally coming to his senses.

"I pulled up. Woodsy gestured for me to roll down the window. He pointed at his car saying, 'How rude of me! What was I thinking? Would you like to come in for a while?'"

Therapist Jeanene Tichenor, "I teach people to laugh in the middle of fear. I worked with a husband and wife who kept coming in with the same problems. They never followed through with any of the solutions we agreed on. For weeks this went on with no change.

"During one afternoon session, the wife pulled a gun and threatened to shoot her husband. I laughed. The shocked woman asked what was so funny.

"I said, 'You never follow through with anything. I'm sure you won't with this either.'

"She put away the gun. We continued our session with no interruptions."

Patrick Murray *is a master ventriloquist. He's six-foot, two inches tall, and white. One puppet he uses in his act is a black Jamaican puppet named Matilda. Patrick's Jamaican accent is so authentic that Jamaicans enjoy Matilda's character more than anyone.*

Patrick, "I was going through customs in Montego Bay to board a cruise ship. A Jamaican official was looking through my bag, saw a couple of the puppet heads and said, 'Oh my God, this is something bad.'

"I explained I was a ventriloquist. He didn't understand. The official kept searching my bags. I was afraid I might miss my ship or even end up in jail.

"After 20 minutes, I reached into the bag and pulled out Matilda. I put her right in the official's face and said in a perfect Jamaican accent,

"'Hello, my darling.'

"The customs official stepped back and said, 'Oh my God, she's Jamaican.'

"Matilda and the customs official started having a conversation – never acknowledging it was me doing the talking. They were becoming fast friends.

"I had Matilda call the customs official closer and whisper, 'See this big, white "mon" behind me? He knows some Wicked VooDoo.'

"I was through customs in seconds."

USAF Major Wes Schierman,

"The North Vietnamese had been threatening to execute POWs as war criminals. June 1966, a group of us were taken from a camp in North Vietnam. We were handcuffed, blindfolded, placed in trucks and driven 40 miles to Hanoi. Many of us felt this would be a one-way trip.

"When the trucks stopped and our blindfolds were removed, we found ourselves in Hanoi Stadium. Thousands of screaming Vietnamese filled the stands. Our silence was broken when a young Navy captain said, 'The Christians are here. Where are the lions?' As serious as our situation was, we laughed.

"That evening, we were joined by 38 more POWs from the Hanoi Hilton. We were paraded through the streets of Hanoi. The Vietnamese people were allowed to demonstrate their hatred for us. We were cursed at, spit-on, beaten, cut by rocks, glass, bricks and bottles. After an hour, we literally had to fight our way back to Hanoi Stadium.

"As we fell to the ground, exhausted, Navy Lieutenant Cole Black, who had only been a POW for a week said, 'Do you guys do this very often?'

"It hurt to laugh, but we did it anyway."

Charley Plumb was a prisoner of war in Vietnam for over 2,700 days. Charley was tortured and nearly beaten to death for information. Sometimes he was beaten because his captors got drunk and thought it was fun.

The first time he was tortured, Charley lay on the cold concrete floor, barely able to open his eyes. Before he passed out from the excruciating pain, he smiled. Scrawled along the base board of a wall he read:

"Smile! You're on Candid Camera!"

Chapter 7

Depression
&
Suicide

Randy, "I attempted to kill myself several times. This last time, I saw Jesus. He told me to go back. It wasn't my time yet.

"The funny thing is, I'm Jewish.

"Since that moment, I find humor everywhere. It gets me through the day."

Managing our emotions

is vital to living a joyful life.

Emotional Problems

Problems are situations that are unwelcome or harmful. They need to be dealt with and fixed. One of the most challenging problems is our emotions.

Depression

... is a BIG emotional problem. It can be explained as a state of low spirits, loss of hope, sadness, feeling inadequate, or loneliness.

Depression IS a problem to be solved. It is a treatable providing the following are done:

1. Admit you are depressed
2. Identify your sadness
3. Understand your emotions
4. And be willing to

Manage your Depression

HUMOR & DEPRESSION

WHEN we know the trigger points that sink us into depression.

WHEN we feel no shame about who we are and what we've been through.
WHEN we understand our emotions.

AND

WHEN we can find the HUMOR and LAUGH at ourselves & thoughts - we become superior to our depression. It doesn't control us anymore. We CONTROL it. And our Depression is now MANAGEABLE!

David

Sarah decided to end her life. She parked her car in the garage, closed the door and left the motor running.

Sarah, "The next morning, I woke up realizing I was still alive. Not only that, I was out of gas.

"While walking to the service station, I realized that the good Lord must want me to stick around."

Nancy, "My best friend, Julie's, brother was very frugal. Sadly, he killed himself. A month after the funeral, Julie called. She was laughing. While going over her brother's bills, she found a receipt for the gun he used to kill himself. He charged it. And it was on sale."

Laughter & Humor
may be that missing piece
for joy to return.

Mary appeared to have it all together.
She was upbeat, funny and outrageous.
She was a pillar of strength.
One day, she collapsed.

Mary, "I was committed. When they told me I was going to a mental ward, I cringed. But deep inside, I knew I needed to be there. One patient helped me get on the right track. I was depressed, eating in the lunchroom, alone. A guy I didn't know sat across from me. Without an introduction, he said, 'Look. You're nuts. I'm nuts. Everybody's nuts.'

"'We just got caught.'"

Susan Kaple,
"I was the mother of twins Scott and Matthew. At the age of 14, Matthew died. As we were sitting Shiva and talking Scott said,

"'Mom remember when I made Matt cry when I told him he was adopted?'

"Then I said, 'Yes, and remember when I said, 'Yes that's true and do you know how hard it was to find a kid who looked exactly like you?'"

> **Susan found her eight-year old son face down in a pond.**

He still had a pulse and they rushed him to the hospital. As her husband waited with their son in ICU, Susan went to the cafeteria to get some coffee.

She sat by herself at a table next to another table with four nurses laughing. The nurses invited Susan into their conversation. They were talking about their kids and the funny things they do. There was no mention why Susan was at the hospital.

One of the nurses asked Susan if she had any kids. Susan told her she had eight. That nurse said, 'Oh my, if I had that many kids I'd have to drown one of them – and all of the nurses started laughing.

Susan, "I didn't tell them. I thought, what are the odds someone would ever say that?

"I realized that God had just given me a gift.

"I had a choice, I could get depressed, mad, or realize the absurdity of that moment. I chose to find the humor. Oh, I wasn't laughing outwardly – it was an inner chuckle that really helped.

"My son did die. It was obviously quite sad. I never suffered any depression. And it was because of that moment I remembered what the nurse said and my choice to find the humor.

"It's important to understand there was nothing funny about my son dying. What was humorous was that none of the nurses had any idea why I was at the hospital that day.

"Every time I think back to that moment, I smile. And that smile is what helps me from getting depressed. And the truth is, my son had a great sense of humor.

He would have laughed at that too.

In the middle of a tense divorce, the husband returned to the house to pick up the last of his possessions.

Before walking out the front door he turned, looking at his soon-to-be ex-wife.

Man, "I know this has been difficult for you. It's been kind of tough for me, too. After this is all over, do you think we can still have sex?"

      She looked at him in amazement

Woman, "Sure we can. Just not with each other!"

      She smiled and shut the door.

◤ Epilogue of this story

Weeks before the husband came to
get his clothes, the woman was going
through serious depression. She had
a hard time getting out of bed. After
she slammed the door in his face, she
called her friends and mom. Every
time she told them what she did
- she started laughing. All of that
laughing helped her move through
her divorce and helped her dissolve
her depression.

David

John Shucart suffered from depression for over 50 years. At age 58, he was in a serious automobile crash that left him in excruciating pain. All of the medicine John took not only didn't relieve his pain, he got addicted to the medication.

John had reached the end of the rope. He decided he was going to end his life. He was going to asphyxiate himself in his car. He didn't want to do it at home and have his wife and kids find him.

John called rental garage companies to find a place to kill himself. As he called around, John found himself negotiating for the cheapest place to rent. After the third call, John hung up. He began laughing. Then John called his friend Eric and told him he wanted to end his life. Eric immediately drove over to John's house.

When John told Eric what he had been doing, calling the rental companies, the two men started laughing uncontrollably. After the men stopped laughing, John said to Eric,

"I don't really want to kill myself. I just want to feel like this – happy and pain free."

The importance of a trusted friend.

One of the most important things for anyone suffering from depression is to have someone to talk to whom you trust. When you share your feelings, thoughts, frustrations and disappointments with a trusted confidante - your buried thoughts and feelings come out.

And when you laugh and find the humor together, something incredible happens. There is fellowship of joy that connects your collective souls.

David

Chapter 8

Death & Grief

Momento Mori

Trappist Monks, aren't saddened or frightened by death. They greet each other with, "Momento Mori" – remember you're dying. They keep in their thoughts they're mortal. This daily reminder leads to a life of meaning – appreciating every precious second.

It is with passion and reverence I offer you a new way of thinking – the possibility of finding humor in what scares us the most – DEATH

You may not be ready to laugh at death. I understand. This chapter is available whenever you are.

Before I ever heard of a Trappist Monk I wouldn't have believed that death could be the meaning of life. I do now!

David

Hospice Workers

"If we don't understand death, we cannot understand life. The way we live is the way we die. We have to be careful to not exclusively put a spiritual realm around death, forgetting the dying person's humanity. That's why it's so important to know about my patients – because that's where the grief is.

"Grief is the life a person is giving up. While we embrace sadness and fear, we must never forget to laugh. Humor is part of our humanity.

"To laugh and experience joy in critical moments is crucial to our lives. We are not created to be sad sacks."

– Sister Loretta Maguire

Hospice nurse,
"I was wearing scrubs when I picked up my daughter, Megan, from school. One of her friends asked, 'What does your mommy do?'

"'She's a nurse,' Megan said. 'And all of her patients die.'"

Charles,
"My first job as a volunteer was to model for the new brochure. Since I'm in my 70s, I looked like a patient. The photographer had me get in bed and wait while he went to get some equipment.

"A new nurse came on duty and saw me in bed.

"'Oh, I see we have a new patient. Do we need an enema?' she said.

"You wouldn't believe how fast I got out of that bed."

Hospice Nurses

Hospice Nurse Marta,
"I have to laugh. It's the healthiest way to survive the doom and gloom of death."

Nurses aid,
"You have to laugh with the family that misunderstood when I said we needed new bedding. The next day, the four sons carried in a new bed."

Nurse Patty,
"I asked a 102-year-old woman if she was afraid to die.

"She said, 'No, I'm ready to go.'

"'Is something stopping you?' I said. 'You know you'll probably meet your late husband.'

"'That's what's stopping me,' she said."

Nurse Debbie,
"Hospice humor? You've got to be kidding! Death and dying? That's serious stuff. What could you laugh at in a hospice? But you learn to laugh.

"You laugh with a co-worker who complained about a foul odor and later found a dead mouse in her pocket – put there by a patient as a practical joke.

"You laugh at a teaching session demonstrating proper procedure for changing a roll of toilet paper.

"You learn laughter relieves pain like medication, but with far fewer side effects.

"You learn laughter adds life to the days of a dying patient.

"You learn the most deadly of all life-threatening conditions is the absence of laughter. Yet, this condition is curable, simply by learning to laugh."

Cindy, "For several years my brother-in-law has lived on the streets of Arizona. During that time he was hit by a bus and brought back to life. A few years later he had a liver disease from too much alcohol. He was hospitalized. During that time his heart stopped. Again, he was brought back to life.

"A week ago, he was walking across the street and had a seizure. He was run over by a car. It killed him.

"As I sat with my mother-in-law, she restated the times about how he died and came back. I snickered.

"She said *'What's so funny?'*

"*'Third time's a charm,'* I said.

"She laughed and said,

'That's why I keep you around.'"

Uncle Al lay dying in hospice. The entire family was gathered in his room – all 17 of them. His 87-year-old wife walks in the room and asks,

"Al, do you know who I am?"

He looked around the room, smiled and said,

"Take your clothes off and I'll see."

Chaplain Greg,

"The nurse told me Sally was awake even though she was totally unresponsive. She didn't move. She didn't open her eyes. She didn't speak.

"When I recited the Lord's Prayer, she didn't respond. I read the 23rd Psalm; no reaction. Finally, I started singing Amazing Grace. My voice isn't very good, but it didn't matter. Sally seemed to stir, so I sang the second verse even louder.

"When I started the third, Sally opened her eyes. She turned to me and said,

"'Please … stop.'"

Nurse Judy cares for dying patients and counsels families of the terminally ill.

Judy, "Fran had been suffering from a chronic illness. Her daughter, Sue, had been her primary caretaker. I told Sue, 'When your mom is ready, tell her to go toward the light.'

"Fran's vitals were diminishing rapidly, but she would not let go. Sue was exhausted and emotionally drained.

"One evening, I heard whispering in Fran's room. I peeked in. Sue was shining a flashlight on the ceiling, whispering to her mother, 'Go to the light. Go to the light.'

"I ran away snorting with laughter."

Greta,

"**G**randpa died in his house. Our family was there. We joined hands and began praying. At this solemn moment, the phone rang.

"Nobody stopped to answer. We continued to pray. The loud ring filled the house. On the ninth ring, the answering machine went off. It was grandpa's voice, of course; it was his house.

"We all heard grandpa say, 'Hi. I'm not here right now. If you leave a message I'll try to get back to you, but I'm not sure when that will be.'"

Herman

"I may be 101 years old, but I got news for you, I ain't beating death. Far as I can recollect, the death rate is, and will always be 100%. There ain't no cure and no doctor can fix it.

"So what am I going to do about it? Go have some strawberry ice cream and a snickerdoodle.

"How do you think I made it this long?"

Why is it easy for some to find
humor in tough times?
They already think funny.

Why is it harder for others?
They don't.

David

Judy, "When my dad moved to the hospice house, I stayed with him most of the time. One night, my sister relieved me so I could get some sleep. I left around 10 at night. One hour later, my sister called. She told me to come back immediately. Dad wasn't doing very good. He died an hour later.

"After the funeral home took dad, we sat in silence. I started laughing. 'What's so funny?' my sister asked.

"'You know,' I kept laughing, 'dad did a lot better when he was with me.'"

Funeral director,

"While a woman was pre-planning her funeral, she nonchalantly told me she was flat-chested and to make sure she was facing the right way in her casket.

"A month later, she died. When I began preparing her for the funeral, I started laughing. Written on her chest in magic marker was, 'This side up.'"

DEATH is a fact.
It's going to happen no
matter what. Running from
it, choosing not to accept it,
won't make it go away.

Choosing to understand
and face it eases our
thoughts when the time
comes.

When we peacefully accept
our own death; it is then, we
truly begin to live.

David

When someone you love dies or is dying, you get sad, even mad. Why shouldn't you? If there's a time to be emotional, that's it.

And that's healthy.

Grief only becomes unhealthy when it gets out of control. A snowball of sadness can turn into an avalanche of grief that will bury you alive.

Humor stops that momentum, freeing you to move on with your own life.

David

Chaplain Steve Smith, "The deceased wrote her own eulogy and asked that 'Somewhere Over the Rainbow' be played at the conclusion. While reading this glowing eulogy, I noticed people giving each other puzzled looks. Apparently, the dearly departed wasn't quite as wonderful as she thought.

"At the conclusion of the speech I said, 'And this is how she wished to be remembered.'

"At that sensitive moment, 'Somewhere Over the Rainbow' from 'The Wizard of Oz' was supposed to play. But someone pressed the wrong button. 'Ding-Dong, the Witch is Dead' came over the sound system instead."

"Laughing at death is like owning a car. A car, like us, will one day quit running. But we must never stop enjoying the ride.

"Sometimes the journey is bumpy, causing numerous stops. Other times it's fun and easy. Either way, we keep driving.

"When we find humor and laugh at death, it doesn't mean we're irreverent. It means we are navigating through life's toughest road by enjoying the funny detours."

David

More from the good Chaplain

Chaplain Steve, "It's okay to have fun at funerals. After all, the first three letters of funeral are f-u-n.

"A woman insisted on being cremated. She wanted her ashes spread on her vegetable garden, just so I would say at her funeral, 'She was one hot tomato.'

"At another funeral, the family made a picture board of their departed husband and father. One photo showed him dancing with his wife. 'Thank goodness you're Methodist,' I said. 'If you were Baptist, he wouldn't get into heaven.'

"At another memorial service, I began, 'Our lost loved one, Jack, is still with us today. Right here, right now.' Pointing at the casket, I said, 'And I'm not talking about Jack-in-the-box.'

"The family, stunned, started laughing. I was relieved they thought it was funny, too."

Simply evoke a pleasant memory

Rabbi Alan Cohen, "When I conduct a funeral, I choose my words carefully to evoke a pleasant memory of the departed – many times humorous. My intention is not to be a comedian. I have learned that the people in attendance, especially the family, appreciate those funny memories. Here are two examples:

"One man was late his entire life. During his eulogy I said, 'This day, he was finally on time.'

"At another service, I said of a woman, 'She would never, ever let me get the last word. Today, I will.'"

Tim's grandmother died in her house. Upon hearing the news, the entire family immediately went to grandma's house. Tim's five-year-old niece was there.

Everyone called grandma, 'Grandma Birdie' because she had a pet parakeet which she kept in her bedroom and always talked to. As the family gathered around grandma's bed, Tim's niece went over to the birdcage and began feeding grandma's bird.

The feeling in the room was somber. The minister began to pray. People joined hands and some began crying. At this sacred moment, Tim's niece screamed, "Ouch!"

The family turned toward the cage and heard the little girl say to the bird, "Why'd you bite me? I didn't kill her."

Opening up that window of humor

Jim Fussell's dad, Jerome, was an expert on proper grammar. He worked as an editor for Webster Dictionaries.

Jim, "Dad was on his deathbed, with just a few hours left. My sister, Nancy, ran in the room with her husband.

"'Daddy, I am so sorry John and me didn't get here sooner. What can we do?'

"Dad motioned with his frail hand, calling her closer. With Nancy's ear next to his lips, dad whispered, 'John and I.'

"That was my dad. What a great way to remember him."

Carl, "Dad was very sick. One of his favorite possessions was a talking watch. The timepiece would call out the hour, on the hour. Dad loved it.

"One day I went to see him. When I walked in his house, dad looked like he was sleeping, so I didn't disturb him. Then I noticed his medication was sitting out. I went over to check on him, saw he was dead and immediately called 911.

"The paramedics asked if I wanted to try resuscitating dad. I declined. He was in no more pain.

"They covered him with a sheet and began their paperwork. One of the paramedics asked for the exact time of death. From under the sheet, dad's watch proclaimed, 'One o'clock pm!'

"The paramedics nearly jumped out of their shoes."

"We're not laughing to be irreverent."

Beverly Jamison, "When my sister Shirley died, my brother Warren and I decided to spread her ashes on the farm where we were born. As we scattered her remains over a meadow of wildflowers, a lump fell to the ground.

"Warren kicked it, saying, 'There you go sis, one last kick in the ash.'

"We laughed so hard we had to hang on to each other so we wouldn't fall over. Shirley would have loved it."

"We're laughing to not stay sad."

Millie, "My husband, Bud, died. At the gravesite, my daughter and I stood before the open grave, waiting for the casket, family and friends to arrive. We were crying uncontrollably. I told my daughter we must compose ourselves before the others arrived. She told me she would say a prayer. With heads bowed and tearful eyes, she said,

"'Dear God, this Bud's for you.'"

Dick Solowitz, "A man with Parkinson's disease was delivering my father's eulogy. As he read, his hands were shaking so bad he messed up the names and relations. This made my brother and me laugh. I whispered. 'I want this guy for my funeral.'

"My brother shot back,

"'You'd better go before next week.'"

Paulette, "Dad was 64 and didn't have long to live. As he lay in bed, Betty Carole, his high-school sweetheart walked in the room. She said hi to us then crawled in dad's bed.

"'George,' Betty Carole said, 'after all these years you finally got me where you want me – in bed with you.'

"'Betty Carole,' dad said, 'you got me at a most unfortunate time. The only thing that works in my pants is my pocket-knife.'"

JD, "After my father died, I used humor to work through the loss. People asked what my father did and I would smile and say, 'Nothing, he just lays around and makes an ash out of himself. When I told them he was cremated, they got uncomfortable. That made me laugh even harder.

"Three years ago my mother died. She lost her battle with depression. She took her own life. I found out this was her third attempt. The doctor who told me had no idea of my sense of humor. When he asked me what I thought, I said, 'Well it's just like our family to start a project and not finish it.'

"I laughed. Because if you don't, it will build and become far worse. I love my parents with all my heart for giving me my sense of humor and teaching me to cope with life and all that it throws at me."

Mary, "My husband died. After the funeral my family was at our house. It was very sad. We were gathered in the living room and there wasn't much talking.

"My five-year-old grandson walked into the room holding my husband's false teeth.

"'Oh my God,' he said, 'grandpa went off to heaven and forgot his teeth.'"

Judy,

"My dad was a big guy. I'm talking over 6'5 and close to 300 pounds. When he died, he was cremated. At the funeral home the Funeral Director handed me the urn with dad's ashes. In front of the entire family I shook it and said,

"Dad, you lost some weight."

Bill Miller, "My 76-year-old mother lived a few blocks away from us. When she did not answer the phone one day, I found her at home on the floor. I tried to resuscitate her. It didn't work.

"She wanted to be buried back home in Pennsylvania. We had her body embalmed and placed in a casket in Albuquerque. Before flying her home, I went to the funeral parlor to see her.

"The undertaker said, 'Please let me know if there are any minor adjustments. If you want your mom's front bangs to lie differently let us know.'

"I started giggling. In my head I was hearing the airline announcement, 'Please be careful when opening the overhead compartments because the contents may have shifted during flight.'

"That would have made mom laugh. The more I thought of it, the funnier it became. It was the beginning of my healing.

"The funniest part – when we opened her casket in Pennsylvania, sure enough, mom's bangs had shifted off of her forehead."

Five-year-old Jarod's grandma died. They had a very close and special relationship.

At the funeral, he stood next to his grandma's casket holding on like he was holding on to her hand.

It was time for the service to start. Jarod's mother came up to him and said,

"'Honey we have to sit down now. Your grandma is dead.'

"'I guess so,' Jarod said, "she's been in that box for over 3 days.'"

Funeral Director - George Aliotta

" I just took care of a funeral. The family requested we take the hearse by the deceased's home then on to the cemetery. The hearse driver said he knew where the house was and not to worry. The family limo followed us.

"As we were driving and driving the driver turns to me and admits he's lost. We ended up on a dead-end street. I had him stop the hearse. I was going to apologize and tell the family the truth; we were lost.

"As I walked back to the family car, one of the family got out of the limousine laughing uncontrollably. When I began apologizing for getting lost he said,

"'This is the best ending to my dad's life. Anywhere my father drove, he always got lost. Now, our entire family knows that dad is with us this morning. He would have wanted us to laugh and not cry."

Let joyful memories help grief

Ron,
"My dad was an avid car man. He loved his '52 Buick. He worked on it all the time – and did for years.

"A few hours before dad died he called me to his bedside. He couldn't speak but he could write. "On a sheet of paper he wrote:

Change oil for Buick

"I wrote:
10W40 Valvoline?

"Dad wrote:
Yes and get the free car wash."

Minister Harry Strong

"I was to conduct a funeral at 11:00 a.m. for a woman named Lucille. Walter, the Funeral Director called at 9:30 telling me the funeral had been postponed. He would call when it was rescheduled. I got no explanation what happened.

"I found from Lucille's family what happened. Their family arrived at the funeral home at nine o'clock to pay their final respects. That was not their mother in the casket. But it got worse. They buried their mother the day before in another dress, in another casket, at another service, with another family!

"My first thought was, 'This is horrific, but at least they didn't cremate her.' And even though their's was an open casket service, the other family never said a word that it wasn't their dearly departed.

"The next afternoon I get a call that Lucille's service is set for Saturday at 2:00 p.m. Saturday afternoon, I arrived at the funeral home about 1:30 p.m. Walter greeted me and said crying, 'This has been the worst week of my life. I know I'm going to get sued. If this gets out, I'll probably have to close up my business!'

"I said, 'Let's just go inside and try to give Lucille's family as much comfort and support as we possibly can. The rest, will work out in time.'

"I went into the funeral home and greeted the family. Fortunately, Lucille was present. The service went beautifully.

"A few weeks later I asked Walter if he had heard from Lucille's family or her attorney.' He told me no, not yet anyway. He also told me he didn't charge them a dime. Then I asked him about the other family's reaction.

"Walter laughed and said, 'The other family was more than gracious when I explained what had happened.' The son of the departed said, ' Well, honestly, that explains a lot. We thought Mother looked better than she had in years!'

"There was another silver lining Walter told me – actually, a blue lining. The other family had made pre-arrangements for their mother's service including the casket and the lining. They requested a blue lining, but when their mother expired, we could only find that particular casket with a rose lining.

"So when we buried her the first time, well, not really her, but Lucille, we used the casket with the rose lining. But, when we buried her the second time, we had the casket with the blue lining in stock.

So they were very pleased!"

Chapter 9

The Benefits of Humor & Laughing

LAUGHTER

Dr. Michael Miller is the Director for the Center of Preventive Cardiology at the University of Maryland Medical Center.

Dr. Miller, "Mental stress is associated with impairment of the endothelium, the protective barrier lining our blood vessels. This can cause a series of inflammatory reactions that lead to fat and cholesterol build-up in the coronary arteries and ultimately to a heart attack.

"Laughter, along with an active sense of humor, may help protect you against a heart attack.

"Exercising, not smoking and eating foods low in saturated fat will reduce the risk of heart disease. Regular, hearty laughter should be added to the list.

"People with heart disease are less likely to recognize humor or use it to get out of uncomfortable situations. They generally laughed less even in positive situations. They displayed more anger and hostility."

LAUGH
Like your life depends on it!
Because it does

LAUGHING
for 20 seconds
is worth
3 minutes
of
rigorous
exercise.

Dr. William Fry

The physical act of laughing has an immediate impact on the body. The brain is stimulated into greater alertness, enhancing memory and sociability. Laughter increases the concentration of antibodies circulating in the blood stream.

A person who laughs a lot is more resistant to developing infection and other illnesses.

"The stimulation of laughter increases our circulation – benefitting the heart and lowering blood pressure. Laughter increases our respiratory exchange. It also increases our metabolism and activity of our muscles.

Laughing for 20 seconds gives the body the kind of workout you would get from 3 minutes of rigorous exercise.

More Benefits of LAUGHING

In the 1980 New England Journal of Medicine, Dr. Franz Ingelfinger estimated that 85% of all human illnesses can be cured by systems already present in our bodies.

A healing agent called Immunoglobulin A, is produced by our immune system. These IgA cells are the body's first line of defense. They attack foreign organisms, protect us from respiratory problems and have been proven to destroy tumor cells and viruses.

The presence of IgAs varies according to our moods. People with a well-developed sense of humor have been proven to have increased concentrations of IgAs.

The American Journal of Medical Sciences, December 1989, states there is a direct connection between stress, high blood pressure, muscle tension, and immunosuppression – the inhibition of the immune response.

Laughter stimulates the immune system, off-setting the effects of stress by lowering serum cortisol levels and increasing the amount of activated T lymphocytes.

Laughing
benefits us physically

Humor
benefits us emotionally

The Emotional Benefits of HUMOR
(Thinking Funny)

1. We stop thinking about what SCARES us.

2. We quit thinking about our PAIN.

3. We stop thinking about our SADNESS.

4. We quit thinking about our ANGER.

5. Humor makes us laugh.

6. Laughing makes us feel good.

The Emotional Release
of
Physically LAUGHING

When we laugh at something funny, what happens inside of us are the physical benefits previously mentioned. And most importantly - it makes us feel good. Part of that great feeling is we are releasing pent-up emotions of fear, anger and sadness. And that makes us feel even better - giving a fresher approach to any TOUGH TIME.

When a TOUGH TIME happens
we get confused and scared.
We ask ourselves;
What am I suppose to do now?
How do I get through this?
Will I ever get to a good time?

That is what this manual offers -
how to get from a bad time to a
good time. And there are five
underlying factors in all of the
stories you just read that got
these folks through their
TOUGH TIMES.

1. Choice
2. Intention
3. Laughing at Yourself
4. Happiness
5. Permission

CHOICE

Tough Times produce emotions. Being sad, angry or fearful are honest reactions to illness, injury and death. They are not choices we conciously make when getting a life-threatening diagnosis or finding out the death of a loved one. Choice enters into our emotions when we recognize they are preventing us from living a joyful life. We choose not to stay locked up.

Remember Susan

... the woman whose 8 year-old son drowned. And a nurse said, unknowingly, "If I had that many kids, I would have to drown one of them." And Susan shared, "Every time I think back to that moment, I smile. And that smile is what helps me from getting depressed. I had a choice, I could get depressed, mad, or realize the absurdity of that moment. I chose to find the humor and that keeps me in a good place."

Or Doug who had his legs amputated

His friend, Dave was short and he always teased him about his height. After Doug got his legs amputated because of diabetes, he called Dave and said,

"Hey, I just had my legs cut off but I'm still taller than you."

INTENTION

The use of humor will work if your intention is to lighten a heavy situation. But, the person must know you and your intention.

Remember Brian & Sharon

Sharon, insisted her nose was too big. Brian thought she looked great, but she insisted on a nose job. She woke up in recovery and was in a lot of pain. Brian asked if she needed anything.

She told him to just get her a casket and he said, "Well, at least you can close the lid now."

LAUGHING AT YOURSELF

Remember 72 year-old Emma

... who got pulled over for speeding. She told the officer she needed to use the toliet, but really didn't and he let her go. As she drove off she laughed at her prank. She laughed so hard she went. Then pulled over, not because she wet herself but because she laughed so hard her teeth fell out on her lap

HAPPINESS

Many look for ways to deny their feelings and not deal with them. That's why people overeat, drink, smoke, gamble, watch TV, constantly play video games, etc.… They do these to avoid their uneasy emotions. If we are to manage our emotions we must first recognize them. Then, we must learn how to face them and understand them.

All of this requires the will – followed by the action to do it. No one can do it for us. It takes personal responsibility and the action of doing it everyday.

The key to being HAPPY

Happiness is simply what you choose to think about. So is misery. When you make the choice to think funny, laugh and reflect on the joys in life - happiness will flourish. Your misery will diminish. It's that easy and it's that hard. You have to make the choice.

Give yourself
PERMISSION

The expression:

"YOU JUST HAVE TO LAUGH"

is said when people have used humor during

a tough time. When we find a joyful thought in

the middle of a bad time, sometimes we think

it's irreverent, even wrong. Nothing could be

further from the truth. The fact is, most people

would rather laugh than cry. So when we say,

"YOU JUST HAVE TO LAUGH" we are simply

giving ourselves permission to have a pleasant

thought in a not-so-pleasant time.

We all go through dark times.
Humor and laughter are simply the
window you open to let the light
in. And it's that illumination that
opens our hearts to joy.
    Joy is not humor. Joy is the light
humor & laughter brings in any
dark time.
    Please make the choice to
keep that window open. Let the
divine light of humor and laughter
brighten any dark time you may go
through.

Momento Mori!

David Naster